I

THE IMPORTANCE OF THE ENVIRONMENT

Many years ago, according to a story which remains vividly in my memory by reason of its grim suggestiveness, two small boys were one day sauntering along a country road. The sight of an orchard, resplendent in its autumn glory of red and green and gold, tempted them with irresistible appeal, as it has tempted thousands of other boys before and since. Over the rail-fence they scrambled, up a well-laden tree they climbed, and soon were merrily at work filling their pockets.

But now from a near-by cottage came the man who owned the orchard, and his coming was the signal for a hasty descent. One of the boys made good his escape; the other, less quick-footed, was dragged, a loudly-protesting captive, to the home of the local magistrate.

"More apple-stealing!" this stern functionary exclaimed. "Something must be done to stop it. Let us make an example of this bad boy." To prison forthwith he consigned the luckless youth.

His companion, thankful for his happier fate, returned to his home, his school, and his books. From school he went to college, and afterward took up the study of law, beginning his professional career with a reputation for great intellectual ability and strength of character. In course of time he was made a judge.

As judge he was called on to preside at the trial of a man accused of murder. The evidence of guilt was conclusive, conviction speedy. It became his duty to don the black cap and pronounce sentence of death. But before he did this, he was struck with something familiar in the prisoner's sodden, passion-marked features, made inquiry concerning his early history, and, to his mingled horror and amazement, learned that the wretched man was none other than the happy, buoyant lad who had first felt the heavy hand of the law on account of the orchard-robbing episode in which the judge, now about to doom him to the scaffold, had gone scot-free.

Than this strange chapter in human experience I can at the moment recall nothing that more strikingly suggests and illustrates the dominant theory in modern scientific thought regarding the offender against society. The implication that the contrasting careers of the two boys were largely determined by circumstances over which they had no control, and that it was the brutalising jail experience of the one and the more fortunate upbringing of the other that chiefly accounted for their diverse fates, unquestionably represents the views held by the great majority of present-day students of delinquency and crime. To be sure, there are not a few who would raise the question, "Might not the boy who was caught in the orchard have 'gone wrong' in any event, because of inborn defects?" These are the enthusiasts conspicuous to-day as leaders of the so-called eugenics movement looking to the improvement of mankind on stock-breeding principles—by sterilisation of the "unfit," stricter marriage laws, etc. Nor can it be denied that they have on their side a formidable array of facts which would seem to demonstrate the unescapable fatality of a bad heredity. On the other hand it is equally certain that there is a steadily growing body of evidence giving ever greater support to the opposite view—to the view, namely, that after all the influence of heredity is of quite secondary importance to that of environment in the marring or making of a human life.

Even the facts emphasised by the eugenists themselves sometimes tend, on close examination, to bear out the belief that it is in the surroundings and training of a child rather than in his heredity that the sources of his ultimate goodness or badness are mainly to be found. The history of the notorious Juke family, featured by almost every modern advocate of the "fatal heredity" theory, is a case in point.

The first Jukes of whom anything is known were five sisters of obscure parentage who lived in Ulster County, New York, in the second half of the eighteenth century. At least four of the five took early to a life of vice, and eventually all married and had children. Many years afterward a visitor to an Ulster County jail noticed that among its inmates, awaiting trial on various charges, were six members of one family, including two boys accused of assault with intent to kill. Inquiry showed that the six were directly descended from the oldest Juke girl, and that more than half of their male blood-relatives in the county were likewise in some degree criminal.

Impressed by these facts the jail visitor, Mr. R. L. Dugdale, determined to make a genealogical research into the life histories of as many of the descendants of the five Juke sisters as could be traced. Altogether it was found possible to obtain pretty complete data concerning seven hundred and nine of these, with the following astonishing results:

Of the entire seven hundred and nine, not twenty had been skilled workers, and ten of these had learned their trade in prison; only twenty-two had been persons of property, and of this number eight had lost the little they acquired; sixty-four had been in the county alms-house; one hundred and forty-two had received outdoor relief; one hundred and twenty-eight had been prostitutes, and eighteen keepers of houses of ill-fame; finally, seventy-six were reported as criminals, with one hundred and fifteen more or less serious crimes to their discredit. All this in seven generations of a single family.

Surely one might well be tempted to find here "the most striking proof of the heredity of crime," as Cesare Lombroso did not hesitate to pronounce this sad history of the Jukes. But there is something to be added.

Following the publication of Mr. Dugdale's book, "The Jukes," giving the family record, there came under the care of a charitable organisation an eighth-generation descendant of the oldest Juke sister, a foundling baby boy, cast upon the tender mercies of the world with all the burden of "innate depravity" transmitted from his vicious ancestors. Instead of taking it for granted that he would inevitably come to an evil end, the charity-workers decided to give him the benefit of a refined environment and good family care. Accordingly a home was found for him with a kind-hearted widow, whose own sons had grown to a worthy manhood, and from her for ten years he received the loving and intelligent training which is the birthright of every child.

At the end of that time he had developed into a fine, manly boy, with, however, a somewhat superabundant fund of animal spirits and a tendency to unruliness. It was evident that, owing to her advanced age, his foster-mother could not give him the stricter discipline he now seemed to need, and arrangements were made for his adoption by a farmer and his wife living in a Western State. By them he was again treated with the utmost affection, coupled with more firmness than he had hitherto known. Little by little his unruliness disappeared; he became eager to excel both at school and in the work of the farm, and soon became known as one of the best boys of the neighbourhood. The older he grew the more evidence he gave of possessing a strong moral foundation on which to build his future career. When last heard from by the charitable organisation to which he owed so much, he had struck out for himself, an alert, vigorous, forceful young man, of sterling character, and full of the self-confidence which wins success.

Moreover, Mr. Dugdale himself, in the course of his exhaustive account of the evil ways of the Jukes, calls attention to the case of a fifth-generation descendant, the daughter of a brothel-keeper, and having two sisters who eventually became prostitutes. Nor did it seem at all likely that she would turn out any better than they; for, before she was fifteen, she had been arrested and imprisoned for vagrancy. But, as good fortune would have it, shortly after her release from jail she met, fell in love with, and married a young German, a cement-burner of steady, industrious habits. Taken by him out of her former debasing environment, given a good home and the example of a strong character, she grew to a reputable womanhood, respected and admired by all who knew her.

Many similar instances of the saving power of good surroundings might be cited. "One of the most useful men I know of to-day," testifies Mr. Ernest K. Coulter, formerly clerk of the New York Children's Court, "saw his father murder his mother in cold blood. There was a bad record on her side of the house, too. But a good man saw something in that boy while he was being detained as a witness against his father. As a result of that man's interest, that boy to-day is serving his fellow-men and his country in a most important field."

In Pennsylvania an eight-year-old orphan girl of poor parentage, drudge in a city boarding-house, with no companionship except that of ignorant servants, was heralded in the newspapers as a "prodigy of crime" because she had been caught setting fire to a house. When asked in court why she had done this, she made the frank reply, "To see the fire burn and the engines run." There being at that time no probation system in Pennsylvania, she was promptly sentenced to the House of Refuge, where, like the boy sent to jail for stealing apples, she would be sure to come under the influence of vile associates.

But, more fortunate than the boy of the orchard, this child had an unknown friend at court, Mrs. Hannah K. Schoff, who interceded with the judge and gained his permission to place the little incendiarist in a good home instead of the House of Refuge. Five years afterward, reporting to the International Prison Commission the result of her experiment, Mrs. Schoff was able to declare that this dangerous juvenile criminal had developed into "as sweet, attractive, and good a child as can be found anywhere."

An Italian Camorrist had two sons. The younger, at the age of three, was separated from his father, taken to a distant city, and given a good education. Like the Juke child of the eighth generation he grew to be an exemplary young man. His brother, who remained with the father, became, like him, a man of vice and crime, hated, feared, and despised.

But far more impressive than isolated instances like these are the data now available regarding the outcome of similar experimentation on a large scale. Four years ago the Children's Aid Society of New York—the organisation which took the Juke foundling under its wing—published a report detailing the results of its "placing out" system for a period of more than half a century. The officials of this society have always been imbued with the idea that every child, no matter how bad his heredity, is entitled to the benefit of a good home upbringing, and in accordance with this idea they have, during the period covered by the report, placed twenty-eight thousand children in carefully selected homes, besides finding situations in the country for about three times as many older boys and girls. Most of their wards have been slum children, having back of them a family history of crime, vice, insanity, or pauperism. Nevertheless, the society's officials inform us:

"A careful investigation of the records gives the following results: 87 per cent. have done well, 8 per cent. were returned to New York, 2 per cent. died, one quarter of 1 per cent. committed petty crimes and were arrested, and 2¼ per cent. left their homes and disappeared. These last were larger boys of restless disposition, unaccustomed to country life or any sort of restraint. Some of them struck out for themselves, obtaining work at higher wages, and were temporarily lost sight of, but years afterward we hear of them as having grown up good and respected citizens.... The younger children placed out by the society always show a very large average of success. The great proportion have grown up respectable men and women, creditable members of society. Many of them have been legally adopted by their foster-parents. The majority have become successful farmers or farmers' wives, mechanics, and business men. Many have acquired property, and no inconsiderable number of them have attained positions of honour and trust."

One of the children thus developed was a typical waif of the slums, a ragged urchin loitering in the streets of New York, and sleeping in store-entrances and hall-ways, until one day taken in charge by a kindly policeman. Investigation disclosed that he was a homeless orphan, and until some definite provision could be made for his upbringing he was committed to the city institution on Randall's Island. Thence, after a few months, he was transferred to the care of the Children's Aid Society, which undertook to find a home for him.

In midsummer of 1859, accordingly, he was sent to Indiana with a party of other homeless lads, and was placed with Mr. E. E. Hall, a Noblesville farmer. Two years later, to the mingled grief and pride of his foster-parents, and when not yet fifteen years old, he enlisted in the service of his country, entering the army as a drummer-boy. After the war he went back to the Indiana farm, and, employing his leisure moments to good advantage, prepared for college. In the seventies, equipped with a good education and a well-disciplined mind, he moved farther West. He finally settled in North Dakota, where, after engaging successfully in various enterprises, he became, in 1881, the cashier of a bank.

His thoughts now turned to politics, into which he plunged with great vigour, and with every prospect of success, as he had in the meantime won for himself a commanding position as one of the most popular and trusted men in his community. In 1884 he ran for the post of county treasurer, won his election, and, adding to his reputation by the way he conducted this office, held it continuously for six years. Then higher honours were thrust upon him; for, in the Fall of 1890, "Andy" Burke, the former ragged New York street boy, became Governor Andrew H. Burke, of North Dakota.

Closely paralleling his career is that of another New York child derelict, taken in charge about the same time as young Burke, and, by a curious coincidence, a companion of his in the little party of boys sent to Indiana in 1859 by the Children's Aid Society. The name of this other lad was John G. Brady. Before coming into the keeping of the Society he had been deserted by his father, after the death of his mother. He was just ten years old when Mr. John Green, of Tipton, agreed to give him a home.

And it was a good home that Mr. Green gave him, a home in which he was taught the value of hard, earnest work, and of love for God and his fellow-man. Remaining on the farm until he was eighteen, he then became a school-teacher, saved enough out of his scanty earnings to give him a start at college, and three years later entered Yale. By this time he had made up his mind to devote his life to the twofold cause of religion and social service; and in 1874, having graduated with credit from Yale, he became a student in the Union Theological Seminary. After his ordination he went as a missionary to Alaska, where his labours, both religious and secular, won him a firm place in the affections of the people, and lasting recognition as one of the real makers of that distant Territory. He was appointed governor of Alaska by President McKinley in 1897, and reappointed by President Roosevelt, serving three terms.

Further, the records show that one ward of the Children's Aid Society of New York rose to be a supreme court justice, another became chief executive of a Western city, while a third was elected auditor-general of a State. Two were elected to Congress, nine to State legislatures, and about a score to public offices of less importance. Twenty-four became clergymen; thirty-five, lawyers; nineteen, physicians; sixteen, journalists; twenty-nine, bankers; eighty-six, teachers; seven, high-school principals; two, school superintendents; and two, college professors. Farming, the army and navy, and various mercantile pursuits gave occupation to most of the rest.

Is it to be wondered, in view of such a showing, that most authorities are inclining more and more to find in a faulty environment rather than in a bad heredity the explanation of the boy who "goes wrong"? Not that it is as yet possible, and perhaps it never will be possible, to rule out entirely the idea of the "born criminal." A small proportion of delinquents undoubtedly do show, almost from infancy, an irresistible and seemingly instinctive impulse to evil; but to just what extent this is due to inherited and irremediable conditions remains to be ascertained. Medical progress, indeed, is constantly making it clearer that many supposed instances of "innate depravity" are in reality the result of curable physical defects, and sometimes of defects that are comparatively slight.

To give a typical example, Professor Lightner Witmer, Director of the Psychological Clinic of the University of Pennsylvania, was once consulted about an eleven-year-old boy, of good family, who had been pronounced by several New York specialists "mentally defective" and "certain to prove unmanageable." His father reported that he was unable to do correctly simple sums in addition and subtraction, and could not read a simple sentence without making a number of mistakes; also that he was cowardly, bad-tempered, and quarrelsome. In fine, the statements made concerning him seemed to stamp him as a fit subject for institutional care. But Professor Witmer's preliminary testing caused him to take a somewhat hopeful view of the poor youngster's condition.

"He was," Professor Witmer says, in an interesting report he has made regarding the case (*The Psychological Clinic*, vol. ii, pp. 153–179), "a stocky, well-built, healthy-looking child. He had red hair, and the expression of his face suggested an unsteady temper. The brow was low, but not of a character to awaken a suspicion of mental deficiency. The shape of the aperture of the eyes indicated a possible arrest of fœtal development, but this was the only suspicious symptom. The teeth were in good condition, the mouth closed, the nose undeveloped, the nostrils small. A hasty examination showed the necessity of consulting an oculist, and the appearance of the nose and nostrils called for an examination of the nasopharynx. The chest was fairly well developed, the voice was good, but he had a lisp, and his speech was a trifle thick. Hearing was normal. His manners at table were good. His gait was normal, the knee-jerks were present on both sides, the coordination of the hands was good.

"In his conversation with me and with his family, he seemed to me to be a normal boy of eleven, rather alert mentally, a self-contained, independent sort of boy. If I had visited the family casually, I would not have observed anything wrong with him. My first brief examination was therefore negative, and excepting for the history which the father and mother gave, I should have pronounced the boy normal, but probably suffering from some optical defect and from naso-pharyngeal obstruction."

A more thorough examination confirmed this tentative diagnosis. Although nothing of the sort had previously been suspected, it was discovered that the little fellow was nearly blind in one eye. Also he was suffering from a poor circulation. On the other hand, despite his mental retardation a careful psychological examination showed that naturally he was bright enough. It seemed evident to Professor Witmer, consequently, that the chief cause for the boy's mental and moral defects lay in improper upbringing, plus the eye-strain which had undoubtedly made school work difficult for him, and had in addition been a source of neural irritation. In verification of this, after he had been provided with eye-glasses and given a few months of special training in the hospital school connected with the psychological clinic, the supposedly "feebleminded child" not only made rapid headway when placed in a regular school, but also showed a surprising moral improvement.

Even diseases of the teeth may play no small part in the making of the wayward boy. There was brought one day to Professor Witmer's clinic a youngster who for months had been the despair of his parents. He had got completely beyond the control of both home and school discipline; spent his days idling in the streets; seemed incapable of telling the truth; stole all sorts of small articles belonging to his parents, including his father's watch, which he sold for five cents; and had even begun to steal from the neighbours, a weakness which soon brought him into the clutches of the law. Placed on probation by the judge of the juvenile court, he had behaved as badly as ever, until, as a last resort, it was decided to see what the psychological clinic could do for him.

Beyond indications of some slight eye-strain nothing specially abnormal was found in his physical condition until his mouth was examined. Then it was seen that a number of his first teeth had not been shed, and that the second teeth were forcing their way out alongside the old ones, causing the gums to be greatly swollen and inflamed. Taken at once to the dental clinic he was examined more carefully by Dean Edward C. Kirk, who, advising gradual removal of the lingering first teeth, suggested the possibility that when the boy was relieved of all dental stress his conduct would show marked improvement. The outcome fully justified this suggestion. Says Doctor Arthur Holmes, who watched the case closely in all its stages (*The PsychologicalClinic*, vol. iv, pp. 19–22):

"In spite of Harry's rebellion and loudly expressed fear, he was immediately relieved of one outgrown canine tooth. The effect was almost instantaneous. His whole nervous system seemed to express itself in one sigh of relief.... From that time his improvement has been marked and continuous. His teeth were removed gradually as it was found expedient. Closely associated with this dental condition, and possibly aggravated by it, was an eye weakness discovered at the eye clinic. In order to insure proper treatment, Harry was placed in charge of the social worker of the psychological clinic, who saw that the drops were regularly put in his eyes, accompanied him to the eye specialist, and not only secured glasses for him but accomplished the hitherto impossible feat of making him wear them.

"On account of the dental work and the refraction of his eyes, he was not sent back to public school. Through the psychological clinic a private school was found where the boy could receive the intelligent and sympathetic training he needed. His whole demeanour under the private instruction has been that of a normal boy. He has been put upon his honour and trusted in numberless ways, and in every case he has justified the expectations of his teacher. He is now a healthy boy, with a boy's natural curiosity, with good manners, good temper, with no more than the average nervousness, and with every prospect of taking his proper place in society and developing into an efficient and moral citizen."

A still more remarkable case that has recently come to my knowledge concerns a Cleveland youth who, up to the age of sixteen, had been a model of good conduct. Then, having gone through high school and begun work with a business firm, he suddenly developed thieving tendencies, finally breaking into a post-office, an exploit which earned for him a term in a reformatory. This was so far from curing him that soon after his release he adventured into highway robbery, was caught, and was sent to jail.

So sudden and startling had been the change in his behaviour that the Cleveland police authorities were convinced he was not responsible for his actions, and advised his mother to have him committed to an asylum for the insane. Before taking this extreme step she had him examined by a neurologist, Doctor Henry S. Upson, whose careful testing of the boy failed to disclose any signs of organic brain trouble. Dr. Upson noticed, however, that his teeth were badly decayed, and this led him to suggest an X-ray examination, as a result of which it was discovered that the youthful criminal was suffering from several abscessed and impacted teeth.

Following an operation for their removal, there was a steady improvement in his moral as well as his physical health. When his term of imprisonment was at an end he found work in a printing-shop, and at last accounts, a year after the operation, had won for himself the reputation of being "quiet and industrious, self-controlled, and without any indication of either moral or mental aberration." (*ThePsychologicalClinic*, vol. iv, pp. 150–153.)

In a single institution—the New York Juvenile Asylum—it was found that the degeneracy of 20 per cent. of a group of fifty "bad boys," who were mentally as well as morally backward, was due in great measure to similar trivial physical defects, adenoids, enlarged glands, eye and ear troubles, etc. Not so very long ago these boys, like the boys in the individual instances mentioned, would have been deemed the hopeless victims of a bad heredity. It is therefore fair to assume that in time to come other remediable, but as yet unsuspected, physical causes of imperfect mental and moral functioning will be discovered.

This is not to say that in such cases medication or the surgeon's knife will prove all-sufficient to prevent the transition from "naughtiness" into outright vice and crime. To this end good moral training will still be the indispensable safeguard, and particularly the moral training to be had through the subtle influence of a good home and good associates. Surely as, for example, the results of the activities of the New York Children's Aid Society strongly suggest, the home and the companions of youth are the great determinants of character. As has been so well said by Doctor Paul Dubois, the eminent Swiss physician and philosopher ("Reason and Sentiment," pp. 69–71):

"If you have the happiness to be a well-living man, take care not to attribute the credit of it to yourself. Remember the favourable conditions in which you have lived, surrounded by relatives who loved you and set you a good example; do not forget the close friends who have taken you by the hand and led you away from the quagmires of evil; keep a grateful remembrance for all the teachers who have influenced you, the kind and intelligent schoolmaster, the devoted pastor; realise all these multiple influences which have made of you what you are. Then you will remember that such and such a culprit has not in his sad life met with these favourable conditions, that he had a drunken father or a foolish mother, and that he has lived without affection, exposed to all kinds of temptation. You will then take pity upon this disinherited man, whose mind has been nourished upon malformed mental images, begetting evil sentiments such as immoderate desire or social hatred."

And it is not only the homeless, deserted, or neglected child, allowed to run wild in the streets, drifting or forced into occupations which bring him more or less closely into touch with the ways and haunts of wrong-doing—it is not only this child who is likely in time to become a wrong-doer himself. No less than the neglected child is the "spoiled" one, however good his heredity, apt to degenerate into delinquency, perhaps into criminality of the worst description. In short, to borrow Pascal's pregnant phrase, every child at the outset of his life is a little impulsive being, pushed indifferently toward good or evil according to the influences which surround him.

The blame, then, for the boy who "goes wrong" does not rest with the boy himself, or yet with his remote ancestors. It rests squarely with the parents who, through ignorance or neglect, have failed to mould him aright in the plastic days of childhood. What is needed, especially in this complex civilisation of ours, with its myriad incitements and temptations, is a livelier appreciation of the responsibilities as well as the privileges of parenthood. Most of all, perhaps, from the point of view of coping with the problem of wrong-doing, do parents need to appreciate that it is in the very first years of their children's lives that the work of character-building should be begun.

In this connection a curious story is told of a father and mother, who, full of that sublime eagerness for the welfare of their young which every parent ought to have, took their only child, a handsome boy of three, to an old Greek philosopher.

"We want you," said they, "to take full charge of our child's education, and do the best you can for him."

"How old is he?" the philosopher asked.

"Just three."

The sage shook his head.

"I am sorry," he said, "but you have brought him to me too late."

Modern students of the nature of man are beginning to realise that there is a world of truth in this reply. They are beginning to realise, that, even in the period of dawning intelligence, interests may be created, habits formed, which all the education of later years may not wholly eradicate. Most people, looking back at their years of childhood, are chiefly impressed by the fact that they remember very little of what then happened. Actually, deep in the recesses of their minds, they possess a subconscious remembrance that may be both remarkably extensive and almost incredibly potent in affecting their later development.

The truth of this will become increasingly evident as we proceed. Here let us pause for only one illustrative instance, taken from the experience of one of the most talked about of American women, Miss Helen Keller, who, as is well known, was left by illness deaf, dumb, and blind when less than two years old, but has nevertheless, by careful training, been developed into a woman of brilliant attainments.

Among her many accomplishments not the least astonishing is her power for appreciating music, which she "hears" by placing her hand lightly on the piano and receiving its vibrations. It occurred to Doctor Louis Waldstein, a pioneer in the study of subconscious mental processes, that quite possibly her appreciation of music was connected with latent memories of music she had heard before her illness. To test this theory he obtained from her mother copies of two songs which had often been sung to Miss Keller as an infant in Alabama, but which she had not heard since. These he played in her presence, with a remarkable effect. She became much excited, clapped her hands, laughed, and communicated:

"Father carrying baby up and down, swinging her on his knee! Black Crow! Black Crow!"

It was evident to all present that she had been drawn back in memory to the surroundings of her infancy. But no one knew what she meant by the words "Black Crow," until her mother, in answer to a letter of inquiry, explained that this was the title of a third song which her father used to sing to her.

"What you wrote," commented Mrs. Keller, "interested us very much. The 'Black Crow' is her father's standard song, which he sings to all his children as soon as they can sit on his knee. These are the words, 'Gwine 'long down the old turn row, something hollered, Hello, Joe,' etc. It was a sovereign remedy for putting them (the children) in a good humour, and was sung to Helen hundreds of times. It is possible that she remembers it from its being sung to the younger children as well as herself. The other two

I am convinced she has no association with, unless she can remember them as she heard them before her illness. Certainly before her illness her father used to trot her on his knee, and sing the 'Ten Virgins,' and she would get down and shout as the negroes do in church. It was very amusing. But after she lost her sight and hearing, it was a very painful association, and was not sung to these two little ones" (the younger children).

Almost by itself this impressive bit of evidence justifies Doctor Waldstein's unhesitating declaration, as set forth in his interesting book, "The Subconscious Self":

"In those early impressions of which no one seems to be conscious, least of all the child, and which gather up power as the rolling avalanche, the elements are collected for future emotions, moods, acts, that make up a greater part of the history of the individual and of States, more effective and significant than those that are written down in *mémoires*, however *intimes*, or that can be discovered in archives, however 'secret.' The strange vagaries of affection and passion, which affect the whole existence of men and women—the racial and religious prejudices that shake States and communities to their very foundations, that make and unmake reputations, and set the wheel of progress back into the dark ages—can be traced to such small beginnings and into those nooks of man's subconscious memory."

Decidedly, bearing in mind this principle of the importance of early impressions, the education of the child should be begun while he still is in the cradle—and should in especial include a careful arranging of his environment, both animate and inanimate, so as to put most effectively into play that greatest of all educational forces, "suggestion."

II

SUGGESTION IN EDUCATION

The term "suggestion" has of late fallen into undeserved disrepute. To most people, as a result of its frequent linking with the term "hypnotism," it implies something exceptional and weird. Yet in reality suggestion is one of the most universal of facts, and there is nothing "uncanny" about it. Properly defined it means nothing more than the intrusion of an idea into the mind in such fashion that it is accepted automatically, overcomes all contrary ideas, and leads to a specific course of action. The slightest reflection will show that this is of frequent occurrence.

Every time I yawn after having seen another person do so, I am acting on the suggestion given to me by his action. Every time, after reading a skilfully worded advertisement, I buy something which I do not really need, I am again acting under the influence of suggestion. So, too, when, in a moment of abstraction, I imitate any act perceived subconsciously, as in the amusing instance related by Professor Ochorowitz in his book, "Mental Suggestion":

"My friend, P——, a man no less absent-minded than he is keen of intellect, was playing chess in a neighbouring room. Others of us were talking near the door. I had made the remark that it was my friend's habit when he paid the closest attention to the game to whistle an air from 'Madame Angot.' I was about to accompany him by beating time on the table. But this time he whistled something else—a march from 'Le Prophète.'

"'Listen,' said I to my associates, 'we are going to play a trick upon P——. We will order him to pass from "Le Prophète" to "La Fille de Madame Angot."'

"First I began to drum the march; then, profiting by some notes common to both, I passed to the quicker and more staccato notes of my friend's favourite air. P—— on his part suddenly changed the air, and began to whistle 'Madame Angot.' Every one burst out laughing. My friend was too absorbed in a check to the queen to notice anything.

"'Let us begin again,' said I, 'and go back to "Le Prophète."' And straightway we had Meyerbeer once more, with a special fugue. My friend knew that he had whistled something, but that was all he knew."

Here, obviously, we have on the part of the man accepting and acting on the idea suggested to him, a temporary suspension of the critical faculty. Had he been on the alert, had he been aware of Professor Ochorowitz's intention, he would never have followed the lead thus given, refraining from doing so if only from fear of appearing ridiculous. This element of uncritical, automatic acceptance is fundamental in suggestion, and it is this that makes suggestion such a tremendously important factor in the life of the young.

The child, it has often been said, is the most imitative of beings. This is only another way of saying that childhood is the most suggestible period of life. Precisely because the critical faculty is then undeveloped the child readily accepts and translates into some form of action the suggestions impinging on his mind from the external world. Necessarily some impressions are experienced by him more frequently than others, and by the very fact of repetition these tend to induce in him a more or less fixed mode of reaction. Thus, without the slightest awareness, he acquires good or bad "habits" of thinking and acting, and displays moods and tendencies which, often regarded by parents as quite inexplicable, are the logical and inevitable product of suggestions with which he has been bombarded since his life began.

In this way are to be explained many personal characteristics often mistakenly attributed to the influence of heredity. If a man is a "grouch," and his young son also displays unmistakable signs of grouchiness, it would indeed be rash to jump to the conclusion that the son had been born grouchy. It may well be—the chances are, it is—that he has acquired a grouchy turn of mind simply through imitation of his father's habitual attitude. "A little girl only fifteen months old," to quote one observation by that careful student of child life, B. Perez, "had already begun to imitate her father's frowns and irritable ways and angry voice, and very soon after she learned to use his expressions of anger and impatience. When three years old this child gravely said to a visitor, with whom she argued quite in her father's style, 'Do be quiet, will you? You never let me finish my sentences.'"

Similarly, peculiarities that seem to be wholly physical may thus be handed on from father to child—characteristic gestures with the hands, pursing of the mouth when reading, shrugging the shoulders, etc. Even left-handedness, often conspicuous as a family trait, is probably, in a certain proportion of cases at all events, the result of imitation rather than heredity. In one interesting case cited by Doctor Waldstein ("The Subconscious Self," pp. 56–59), an English lady, Miss X——, had lost her mother when less than three years of age. A year afterward, during her first attempts at sewing, it was noticed that she was threading her needle with her left hand. This had been the habit of her mother, and Mrs. X—— herself continued throughout her life to use her left hand in threading needles, although she was otherwise right-handed.

"Surely," said she to Doctor Waldstein, "this is an example of inheritance, for I could not have been taught to sew by my mother."

When, however, he inquired closely into this lady's mental make-up, he soon discovered that she was most impressionable, easily and unduly affected by her surroundings, full of prejudices, and given to sudden likes and dislikes. Manifestly, if in adult life she was so suggestible, she must have been even more suggestible in early childhood, and Doctor Waldstein promptly asked himself the question:

"Is it not more natural to assume that the mother's habit of threading a needle with her left hand, witnessed daily during the first three years of childhood, left its effect upon the ductile memory of the child, so that she adopted the same habit in the absence of other teaching, than to assume a needle-threading centre on the right side of the brain of this particular individual?"

In view, then, of the extreme suggestibility of childhood, and in view of the fact that under ordinary circumstances the impressions most forcibly impinging on a child's mind are those emanating from his parents, a good parental example is the first essential in utilising the power of suggestion as an aid in education. This may sound trite, but how many parents appreciate all that it involves?

It means the regulation of the whole family life with the special purpose of creating for the child a ceaseless flow of suggestions which, being subconsciously absorbed by him, will give a desirable "set" to his mind. Not merely in their dealings with the child but in their intercourse with one another, with all other members of the family, even with casual visitors, the father and mother will have to be constantly on the alert to manifest only those traits which they desire to see dominant in their little one. If they wish him to be courteous, they themselves must be courteous; if they wish him to grow up industrious, they must be models of enthusiastic industry; if they wish to develop in him sentiments of unselfishness, they must banish selfishness from their hearts.

In a word, they must think and behave as they desire him to think and behave, and, so far as is humanly possible, they must thus behave all the time. This of course necessitates considerable self-restraint and self-training on the parents' part; but it is absolutely indispensable. The child's eyes and ears are always wide open; his suggestibility is such that he is prone to absorb and react to any inconsistency of parental speech or behaviour, no matter how occasional or seemingly insignificant it may be. If the father, in a moment of irritation, eases his feelings by a vigorous expletive, the mother may be horrified next day when her little boy utters a strange-sounding word. If the mother, to avoid a tiresome caller, tells a "white lie" through the maid-servant who answers the caller's ring, neither father nor mother need be astonished if their little girl unexpectedly displays a tendency to untruthfulness; it is not a manifestation of "innate depravity," it is only another illustration of the power of suggestion to affect the growing child.

Even such a "small matter" as the discussion of the news of the day may become a potent factor for evil in the development of the child. There are not a few parents who, entirely unmindful of their children's presence, retail to each other the petty chit-chat, the scandals, the deeds of violence and crime, which so many of our newspapers injudiciously "feature." At the time the child may seem to be paying no heed to the parental discussion; but, if only because it is a discussion between his parents, it is certain to make a profound impression upon him, perhaps to the extent of prompting him to imitate the deeds in question. Hence, in his games, he plays pirate, bandit, train-robber; and sometimes runs away from home and "starts

West," to play bandit and train-robber in earnest. In this way, to the sorrowing parents' amazement, seeds often are unwittingly sown to grow into poisonous plants.

No less mischievous is the discussion, in the child's hearing, of such frequent subjects of conversation as the latest musical comedy or "problem play," the "novel of the hour," the fluctuations of the stock market, the new fashions in gowns, the fortunes of the local professional baseball team. Parents whose interests are thus lamentably limited, or who choose to talk about little else, need not be surprised if their child manifests a colossal indifference to things really worth while. For his sake, if not for their own, they should cultivate an intelligent interest in good books, good music, good art. Discussing these, they will just as surely enlarge his mental and moral horizon, as by discussing inferior themes they will limit it.

And—another point of prime importance—whatever they talk about, they should make it a practice to use only clear, correct language, and should insist on their child doing the same. Above all, they should not converse with him in "baby talk," or permit any linguistic errors he may make to go uncorrected. They should not do this for several reasons, chief among which is the fact that an incorrect diction is itself a great obstacle to correct thinking.

"Language," as one able student of human development, Doctor A. A. Berle, has recently pointed out in his valuable book for parents, "The School in the Home," "is the tool of knowledge. It is the instrument by which we gain and garner information, by which we co-ordinate what we know and make inferences and express results. But if you blunt the tool, not to say destroy it, before you begin to use it, how are you ever to get knowledge in any proper or real sense? Everything depends upon this tool. The mastery of a proper use of the mother tongue is the first and last requisite of sound and extensive mental development. Language is the key to everything that pertains to human life. Once get a language and you have the key to manners, civilisation, habits, customs, history, and all the complex and fascinating story of humanity. Because you get all these things by reading about them, and to read you must know the language and you must know it accurately and extensively, and be able to follow the masters of it who have embodied their great ideas in literature. That process begins almost at the cradle. It begins by cultivating accuracy and skill in the use of the tongue. It begins by striking at, and out, every false thing, the moment it appears."

And, commenting on the special dangers of "baby talk," Doctor Berle justly observes:

"It is not enough that a word be spoken. It makes a great deal of difference how it is spoken. The proper vocalisation of words has an effect upon children, which is often, one may say generally, overlooked. Almost everybody is fond of repeating the baby's efforts to talk, and 'baby talk' lingers in many homes an innocent but costly pleasure, for the parents and the children alike. There are many persons of mature age at this moment who will never pronounce certain words properly, since they became accustomed to a false pronunciation in childhood, because somebody thought it was 'cute.' There are many persons who will never get over certain false associations of ideas, because somebody thought it was very amusing and funny to see the child mixing up things in such a beautifully childlike way."

Putting into practice this first principle of education through the suggestive power of a parental example characterised by correctness of speech, soundness of thought, and the moral qualities of cheerfulness, unselfishness, kindness, politeness, industriousness, and the other virtues, the greatest care must also be taken to "fertilise" the child's mind through proper adjustment of his physical surroundings. Nothing is more certain—and least appreciated by the average parent—than the fact that every detail in the child's material environment is of suggestive significance to him. Even the pictures on the walls of his room, the design and arrangement of the furniture and ornaments, the pattern and colouring of the wall-paper, may play a decisive part in shaping his character and quickening or deadening his intellectual activities. For the matter of that, as observation and experiment have repeatedly demonstrated, adults almost as much as children react to the suggestive influence of their home environment, even to the extent at times of thereby being unfavourably affected in health.

That is why sick people are so frequently benefited by change of scene. Travel removes them from the baneful influence of their accustomed environment, and assists in breaking down the mental habits injurious to their well-being. Too often, however, to their bitter disappointment, they suffer a relapse after returning home. Yet they need not remain abroad indefinitely in order to obtain a lasting cure. In many instances they need not go abroad at all, but can secure the desired result by making a change in their home surroundings. A most instructive case in point is afforded by an experience that occurred to Mr. Frank Alvah Parsons, a practical psychologist as well as a successful teacher of art in New York city.

The mother of one of Mr. Parsons' pupils had long been regarded as a hopeless sufferer from "nerves." She lived in a suburban town, not many miles from New York, but her condition was such that it had been months since she visited that city, and usually she remained at home, secluded in a private apartment, of sitting-room and bedroom.

One day, having occasion to call on her, Mr. Parsons was much impressed with the fact that the furniture and decorations of both these rooms were exceedingly faulty from a psychological as well as an æsthetic point of view. The walls of the sitting-room were hung with mirrors, and the room was fairly smothered with bric-a-brac. In both rooms the colouring and design of the wall-paper contrasted harshly with the floor-coverings, while the furniture, though expensive, was gaudy and inharmonious. He talked the situation over with her daughter, and between them they persuaded her to allow them to make radical alterations in the furnishings of her rooms.

They papered the walls with a soft sage-green paper, without design. The woodwork was made lighter, with a shade of green in it. A brass bedstead was installed, the yellow of the brass blending well with the green of the paper and woodwork. The bric-a-brac was unceremoniously bundled out, and, excepting for a few green draperies and some well-chosen pictures, the rooms were left without ornament. Mahogany furniture, of a quiet, dignified style, replaced the gilded chairs and tables previously there.

The effect was to substitute for the former nerve-irritating environment one that gave out a constant stream of restful, soothing, strengthening suggestions; and the therapeutic value of the change was increased by Mr. Parsons wisely insisting that the patient should not leave the refurnished rooms for two weeks. He desired to expose her, at once and systematically, to the full suggestive effect of her new surroundings. At the end of a month, although she had been told that she would be an invalid for life, she felt strong enough to undertake a shopping expedition to New York, and soon was as well as in her earlier days of robust health.

In this case, of course, the cure was effected at a cost beyond the means of most people. It is not everybody who can afford to refurnish and redecorate his living-quarters. But the point is that everybody can so arrange his environment to begin with as to extract from it suggestions that will assist in maintaining his health and happiness, and in promoting the proper upbringing of his children. This is equally within the reach of a dweller in a Fifth Avenue mansion, a Newport palace, a crowded East Side tenement, or a lonely, isolated farm-house, miles from the nearest village. I might cite many illustrative instances to bear out this statement. Here is one, reported by an observant New York physician:

"The refined tastes and joyous dispositions of the elder children in a family with whom I often came into contact were a matter of some surprise to me, as I could not account for the common trait among them by the position or special characteristics of the parents: they were in the humblest position socially, and all but poor. My first visit to their modest home furnished me with the natural solution, and gave me much food for reflection.

"The children—there were six—occupied two rooms into which the sunlight was pouring as I entered; the remaining rooms of the apartment were sunless for the greater part of the day; the colour and design of the cheap wall-paper were cheerful and unobtrusive; bits of carpet, the table-cover, and the coverlets on the beds were all in harmony, and of quiet design in nearly the elementary colours; everything in these poor rooms of poor people had been chosen with the truest judgment for æsthetic effect, and yet the mother seemed surprised that I could make so much of what seemed to her so simple."

That colours have a profound psychological effect on human beings is a fact which should be appreciated far more generally than is now the case. Used in small quantities, either in the clothing or in household decoration, the colour red, for instance, is most stimulating, both in the way of helping to overcome depression, and quickening the intellectual processes. But when used in any great amount it tends to over-stimulation, with resultant nerve-strain. According to an English savant, Havelock Ellis, who has made a careful study of the psychology of colours, there are some people so constituted that they become violently excited, fall into convulsions, or faint, if obliged even for a short time to look at anything vividly red.

The same effect has been noted from yellow. In one instance, the case of a man operated on at the age of thirty for congenital cataract, it is recorded that "the first time he saw yellow, he became so sick that he thought he would vomit." And that yellow has a nerve-stimulating effect fully comparable with that of red is curiously indicated by the statement of a friend of mine, a professor in a Western university, who says:

"Whenever the day is overcast, or I have to do a piece of work calling for unusual mental exertion, I always wear a red or yellow necktie. I find that either colour has a stimulating effect on my mental processes."

On the other hand, the colour violet appears to have a deadening effect. Another acquaintance, a member of the Harvard University professorial staff, and a well-known psychologist, assures me that the sight of anything violet almost nauseates him, and gives rise to a most depressed feeling. In such a case, however, it may be that the colour is subconsciously associated with some unpleasant occurrence in the earlier life, and that the nausea and depression are merely symbolical manifestations of the presence in the subconsciousness of some memory of this occurrence, concerning which there is no conscious recollection. (This important point will later be discussed in detail.)

Of more immediate significance is the fact that violet rays are sometimes used to quiet unruly patients in asylums for the insane, and that the alienist Osburne, after many years' experience, testifies that "in the absence of structural disease, violet light—for from three to six hours—is most useful in the treatment of excitement, sleeplessness, and acute mania."

Altogether, there is warrant for the assertion that red, yellow, and violet are colours that should not be used overmuch, either in one's apparel or in the decorating of one's home. Blue, green, grey, and brown, on the contrary, have psychological qualities that make them particularly desirable for decorative purposes.

Care must always be exercised, though, to work out a colour scheme that harmonises, since discordant colour effects inevitably carry to the mind suggestions of discordant thinking and feeling and doing. As a first aid to the study of colour harmony—a subject which, as soon as its significance to human welfare is more generally recognised, will be taught far more systematically than at present—I recommend painstaking observation of the colour schemes developed by master artists, as shown in the paintings to be seen in the art museums of our cities; or, better still, excursions into the country, where, in the colour combinations of earth and sky, tree and water, mountainside and valley meadow, one can gain invaluable hints from that greatest of artists, Nature. On such excursions, need I add, the children should be taken along, to receive early lessons in the appreciation of true beauty.

But now, while thus utilising to the full the educational possibilities opened by the suggestibility of childhood—while reinforcing the educational value of example by the educational value of a well-arranged home environment—it must also be recognised that the child's extreme suggestibility carries with it certain dangers. As was said, the essential element in every successful suggestion is the automatic, uncritical acceptance of whatever idea is thus intruded into the mind. It goes without saying that, so long as the critical faculty remains unawakened and untrained, it will always be possible to intrude by suggestion erroneous as well as sound ideas.

More serious still, there is warrant for adding that unless the child's critical powers be developed at an early age—unless he be taught from the outset of his life how to observe accurately and reason closely—the tendency to uncritical acceptance may become more or less of a habit. That, under present conditions of child training, this is a real danger is clearly shown by the results of recent experiments by French and German psychologists.

In Germany, Kosog, visiting a school-room before the beginning of the lesson-hour, placed three objects, a pen-holder, a pocket-knife, and a piece of chalk, so near the edge of the teacher's desk that they could be plainly seen by every pupil in the room. During the brief recess that followed the first lesson-hour, he removed these objects, and after the pupils had reassembled asked them what they had seen on the desk the previous hour. Hardly one of them, it turned out, had noticed the objects at all. Next day, *after leaving the desk entirely bare the first hour*, he put the same question to them at the beginning of the second hour. Now 26 per cent. of the pupils asserted that they had seen the pocket-knife, 57 per cent. the chalk, and 63 per cent. the pen-holder.

In France, the headmaster of a school, following the instructions of the famous psychologist, Alfred Binet, announced to a class of eighty-six boys that he intended to test their memory of the length of lines. A line two inches long, ruled on white cardboard, was shown to each boy, who, after looking at it, had to draw it as accurately as he could on a sheet of paper. The boys were then told that they would be asked to draw another line a little longer than the first, and were accordingly given a second line to copy. In reality it was shorter than the first, being only an inch and three quarters long. Yet out of the entire class only nine resisted the suggestion and believed their eyes and their memories rather than the master's statement. The other seventy-seven boys—some of whom were fourteen years old—made the second line longer than the first.

A variation of the same experiment was made on another class, to whom a series of thirty-six lines was shown, one after the other. Of these lines the first five progressively increased in length, while the remainder were uniformly long. Not one of the forty-two boys who were asked to copy them reached the maximum length at the fifth line, while nine industriously continued making their lines longer up to the last line shown them. The first five lines, that is to say, had acted as a suggestion having sufficient force to induce in them, despite the evidence of their eyes, a belief that the entire series similarly increased in length.

Much the same thing, as everyday observation shows, occurs in the case of full-grown men and women. The judicious have long grieved at the gullibility with which people who are by no means illiterate and uneducated accept and act upon the most preposterous suggestions of the fraudulent advertiser, from the patent-medicine man to the swindling promoter. Political mountebanks and charlatans daily ride into power through nothing else than skilfully working on the suggestibility of the voters. So, too, religious cults, no matter how fantastic, gain a foothold and a following. "I am Elijah," some one announces, and straightway a multitude proclaim him Elijah. "There is no such thing as disease," says another, and thousands take up the cry, accepting the absurd suggestion with as much unthinking readiness as was shown by the French boys who, although they had concrete evidence to the contrary, accepted their master's deceptive statements.

What these, and even more glaring evidences of undue suggestibility, really mean is that there is something wrong with our educational methods. Appreciating this, there is an increasing tendency to criticise and condemn the school system. "Our common schools," exclaims President Emeritus Charles W. Eliot, of Harvard University, "have failed signally to cultivate general intelligence, as is evinced by the failure to deal adequately with the liquor problem, by the prevalence of gambling, of strikes accompanied by violence, and by the persistency of the spoils system." From the standpoint also of mere efficiency much complaint is made. The charge is even heard that the public schools of to-day make for mediocrity, and that instead of fostering they in reality retard the development of a child's intellect. In the words of a recent critic (*The Psychological Clinic*, vol. iv., p. 141):

"The public school attempts the impossible feat of making a course for all children, irrespective of strength, mentality, inheritance, or home environment—whether they are to be lawyers or blacksmiths, artisans or mathematicians. Plainly, this course cannot suit all children. Is it, then, adapted to the bright child? Doctor Witmer, Professor of Psychology in the University of Pennsylvania, says, 'The public schools are not giving the bright child a square deal. He is marking time, waiting for the lame duck to catch up.' Is the course intended to fit the dull pupil? Evidently not, in view of the tears shed by the many who, despite their efforts, fail to keep up to grade.

"It has been suggested that the course has been designed for the average pupil. The 'average' pupil does not exist. You cannot strike an average between a goose and an eagle, nor can you add a dull pupil and a bright pupil together and get anything. A course of study based on this idea is not fitted to any one. Instead, then, of a school to fit the pupil, the pupil is made to fit the school. The lock-step masquerades under the name of discipline. The rigid curriculum tends with each passing year to produce more and more the type of factory employés, obliterating individuality and forcing all into the same mould."

That there is a large measure of truth in these criticisms cannot be denied, and our school authorities to-day are bestirring themselves to effect sundry greatly needed reforms. But is it wholly fair to cast on the schools the blame for human irrationalities of thought and conduct? Nay, is it not possible, in view of the fact that habits are formed so early in life, that the real trouble may be that the material with which the schools have to work—the children of the nation—is more or less unworkable by the time it gets to the schools? Is it not reasonable to assume that neglect of proper instruction in the pre-school period has permitted the formation of faulty and well-nigh unchangeable modes of thinking and feeling?

"But," I hear a puzzled parent protest, "do you mean that the formal education of the child should be begun before he has reached school age? Would you have us lay on the tender mind the burden of actual study?"

I mean precisely that. Not only do I believe that the postponement of formal education to "school age" is a serious pedagogical error, but I also believe that "actual study," properly directed, would by no means prove such a "burden" on the mind of the child as most people take for granted.

I am willing to go further than this, and to contend, for reasons which I shall endeavour to make clear, that if the formal education of children were begun earlier than is the rule at present, and if it were carried out with the supplementary aid of education through a really good example and a really well arranged environment, our boys and girls would develop not only into morally superior men and women, but also into men and women of mental attainments fairly comparable with those to-day displayed by the comparative few acclaimed as men and women of "genius."

III

THE SECRET OF GENIUS

The theory of genius which it is my purpose to present and defend has little in common with the views held by most students of this world-old problem. Especially does it differ from the well-known and at present dominant doctrine of the Moreau-Lombroso-Hagen school of investigators, by whom the man of genius is regarded as an aberrant, even degenerate, type of humanity, closely allied to the insane, and hence by implication deserving to be repressed rather than encouraged. Nor am I at one with those who, justly protesting against the degeneracy theory, themselves contend that genius is an anomaly in the scheme of Nature, and that the man of genius, biologically speaking, is a "variation" dependent on unknown, perhaps unknowable, laws of heredity.

On the contrary, following the lead of the late Frederic W. H. Myers—the first, in my opinion, to glimpse the true significance and fundamental characteristics of genius—I shall endeavour to show that in the man of genius there is, at bottom, no real departure from normality, and that he differs from the "average man" only in being the fortunate possessor of a power for utilising more freely than other men faculties common to all. More than this, going beyond Myers, I venture to affirm that genius is to an appreciable extent susceptible of cultivation, so as to become a far more frequent phenomenon than it is to-day.

In other words, I maintain that God, in giving to the world its Dantes, Newtons, and Emersons, has not intended them as mere objects of admiration and bewilderment, but as indications of possibilities open to the generalty of mankind.

Such a view, it may at once be conceded, could not reasonably have been advanced many years ago. It rests mainly on facts then unknown or misunderstood, and even now little appreciated outside of a narrow circle of scientific investigators. Foremost in importance is the discovery that, in addition to the ordinary realm of conscious thought, there exists in all of us a second realm—that of the so-called subconscious—in which, quite without any will-directed effort of our own, the most varied mental processes are carried on.

The subconscious, in fact, is a kind of vast store-house, wherein are preserved, seemingly without time limit and in the most perfect detail, memory-images of everything we have seen, heard, or otherwise experienced through our sense-organs. It is also a kind of workshop for the facile manipulation of ideas, including even the elaboration of complicated trains of thought. Manifestly, the more freely and habitually one can draw on its resources, the more one ought to be able to accomplish with regard to any set task or chosen field of work. And in this, I am persuaded, we have the clue to the true explanation of the brilliant achievements of the man of genius.

He does what he does so well, not because he is of an abnormal type of mentality, as the Lombrosians ask us to believe, nor yet because he is born with gifts transcending those of other men, but simply because he has found a way more readily, more frequently, and more profitably than others to avail himself of the subconscious powers that are the common heritage of the race. Or, to put it more elaborately in the words of Frederic Myers:

"I would suggest that genius—if that vaguely used word is to receive anything like a psychological definition—should be regarded as a power of utilising a wider range than other men can utilise of faculties in some degree innate in all—a power of appropriating the results of subliminal mentation to subserve the supraliminal stream of thought; so that an 'inspiration of genius' will be, in truth, a subliminal uprush, an emergence into the current of ideas which the man is consciously manipulating of other ideas which he has not consciously originated, but which have shaped themselves beyond his will in profounder regions of his being. I would urge that here there is no real departure from normality; no abnormality, at least in the sense of degeneration; but, rather, a fulfilment of the true norm of man."

That the inspirations of genius are really nothing more than spontaneous upsurgings from the depths of the subconscious, is indeed demonstrable from the recorded statements of men of genius themselves. To the modern psychologist one of the most impressive proofs of the actuality of subconscious mental processes, is the occasional solution in dreams of problems that have long baffled the waking consciousness. In this way abstruse mathematical problems have sometimes been worked out after all hope of solving them had been abandoned; and troublesome clerical errors, the perpetual dread of book-keepers, have been cleared away during sleep, as in the following typical instance, reported by a successful business man to the Society for Psychical Research:

"I had been bothered since September with an error in my cash account for that month, and, despite many hours' examination, it defied all my efforts, and I had almost given it up as a hopeless case. It had been the subject of my waking thoughts for many nights, and had occupied a large portion of my leisure hours. Matters remained thus unsettled until December 11. On this night I had not, to my knowledge, once thought of the subject, but I had not been long in bed, and *asleep*, when my brain was as busy with the books as if I had been at my desk. The cash-book, banker's pass-book, etc., appeared before me, and without any apparent trouble I almost immediately discovered the cause of the mistake, which had arisen out of a complicated cross-entry.

"I perfectly recollect having taken a slip of paper in my dream and making such a memorandum as would enable me to correct the error at some leisure time; having done this, the whole of the circumstances had passed from my mind. When I awoke in the morning I had not the slightest recollection of my dream, nor did it once occur to me during the day, although I had the very books before me on which I had apparently been engaged in my sleep. When I returned home in the afternoon, as I did early for the purpose of dressing, and proceeded to shave, I took up a piece of paper from my dressing-table to wipe my razor, and you may imagine my surprise at finding thereon the very memorandum I fancied had been made during the night.

"The effect on me was such that I returned to our office and turned to the cash-book, when I found that I had really, *when asleep*, detected the error which I could not detect in my waking hours, and had actually jotted it down at the time."

The modern psychological explanation of all this would be that in his many hours of searching through the books he had, though without being in the least aware of it, gradually brought together the data necessary to the solution of his problem; and that in this case this happened to be first definitely formulated in his mind while he slept, thus giving rise to the dream that caused him such astonishment. Or he might from the outset have subconsciously been aware of the cause of his error, but without being able to profit from the knowledge until a favouring condition in sleep permitted its emergence above the threshold of his consciousness.

Now, suppose that instead of being a business man he had been a novelist, artist, or musician, and had been preoccupied with some special or general problem peculiar to his art. If in that event he had had a dream in which was presented to his sleeping consciousness a plot or subject or theme, which, being afterward given permanent form on paper or canvas, proved to have the qualities of a "work of genius," would it not be logical to infer that precisely the same mental processes were operant in the second instance as in the first, the only difference being in the character of the product? This is what, from their own statement, has happened to not a few men of high achievement.

Coleridge's poem "Kubla Khan" was a dream composition. So was the sonata by which the composer Tartini is best known, and to which he appropriately gave the name of "The Devil's Sonata," in recognition of the fact that he owed it to a dream of selling his soul to the devil, and being rewarded by hearing the latter play on a violin the music out of which grew what Tartini himself regarded as his best piece of work. Benjamin Franklin was another man of genius who gained something from his dreams, as was Condillac. But the most striking illustration is afforded by Robert Louis Stevenson, whose marvellous "Doctor Jekyll and Mr. Hyde" was only one of several novels and stories that he conceived in dreams. Stevenson, it is worth adding, in his delightful "Chapter on Dreams," frankly recognises and acknowledges the debt he owed to his subconsciousness, which, with characteristic felicity and whimsicality, he personified as "Brownies" and "little people."

"This dreamer, like many other persons," is the way he puts it, "has encountered some trifling vicissitudes of fortune. When the bank begins to send letters and the butcher to linger at the back gate, he sets to belabouring his brains after a story, for that is his readiest bread-winner; and, behold! at once the little people begin to bestir themselves in the same quest, and labour all night long, and all night long set before him truncheons of tales upon their lighted theatre. No fear of his being frightened now; the flying heart and the frozen scalp are things bygone; applause, growing applause, growing interest, growing exultation in his own cleverness—for he takes all the credit—and at last a jubilant leap to wakefulness, with the cry 'I have it; that'll do!' upon his lips—with such and similar emotions he sits at these nocturnal dramas; with such outbreaks, like Cassius in the play, he scatters the performance in the midst.

"Often enough the waking is a disappointment. He has been too deep asleep, as I explain the thing; drowsiness has gained his little people; they have gone stumbling and maundering through their parts; and the play, to the wakened mind, is seen to be a tissue of absurdities. And yet, how often have these sleepless Brownies done him honest service, and given him, as he sat idly taking his pleasure in the boxes, better tales than he could fashion for himself.

"The more I think of it," Stevenson goes on, "the more I am moved to press upon the world my question, 'Who are the little people?' They are near connections of the dreamer's, beyond doubt; they share in his training; they have plainly learned, like him, to build the scheme of a considerable story, and to arrange emotion in progressive order. Only, I think they have more talent; and one thing is beyond doubt—they can tell him a story piece by piece, like a serial, and keep him the while in ignorance of where they aim.

"That part of my work which is done while I am sleeping is the Brownies' part, beyond contention; but that which is done when I am up and about is by no means necessarily mine, since all goes to show that the Brownies have a hand in it even then."

Than these exquisite paragraphs, it would be hard to find—and I have quoted them for that reason—anything more graphically descriptive of the mechanism which I am convinced is always operant in the production of works of genius. Asleep or awake, it is from the resources of the subconscious region of their minds that men of genius gain the "inspirations" that delight, benefit, or amaze posterity.

Mostly, of course, the subconscious upsurgings come to them when they are awake, sometimes in momentary gleams of insight, sometimes continuing through comparatively long periods, when they write, compose, or develop valuable discoveries without conscious effort. In fact, there even is one type of genius—although by no means the most useful—in which, within a certain limited field, the subconscious is perpetually in evidence, and perpetually responsive to the demands of the upper consciousness. I refer to the so-called "lightning calculators," those prodigies whose mathematical feats, performed without the aid of pencil and paper, have been a source of unending surprise to the world, and have at times been so remarkable as to be well-nigh incredible.

Thus, Zerah Colburn, an American lightning calculator, when only six years old, unable to read, and ignorant of the name and value of any numeral set down on paper, is known to have stated correctly the number of seconds in a period as long as two thousand years, and to have returned the correct answer (9,139,200) to the question, "Supposing I have a corn-field, in which are 7 acres, having 17 rows to each acre, 64 hills to each row, 8 ears on a hill, and 150 kernels on the ear, how many kernels in the corn-field?"

A little later, having been taken by his father to England, it is recorded that, in the presence of a number of witnesses:

"He undertook and succeeded in raising the number 8 to the sixteenth power, 281,474,976,780,656. He was then tried as to other numbers, consisting of one figure, all of which he raised as high as the tenth power, with so much facility that the person appointed to take down the results was obliged to enjoin him not to be too rapid. With respect to numbers of two figures, he would raise some of them to the sixth, seventh, and eighth power, but not always with equal facility; for the larger the products became the more difficult he found it to proceed. He was asked the square root of 106,929, and before the number could be written down he immediately answered 327. He was then requested to name the cube root of 268,336,125, and with equal facility and promptness he replied 645."

Henri Mondeux, Vito Mangiamele, Jacques Inaudi, Zacharias Dase, Jedediah Buxton, Truman Safford, André Ampère, Karl Gauss, George Bidder and his son of the same name, were other world famous calculators. From some of them direct evidence as to the subconscious character of their calculations has been forthcoming. One of the most remarkable in this group, the elder Bidder, in a paper contributed to a scientific journal, declared, "Whenever I feel called upon to make use of the stores of my mind, they seem to rise with the rapidity of lightning." In a later issue of the same journal it is asserted regarding him:

"He had an almost miraculous power of seeing, as it were, intuitively, what factors would divide any large number, not a prime. Thus, if he were given the number 17,861, he would instantly remark that it was 327 × 53. He could not, he said, explain how he did this; it seemed a natural instinct with him."

Another expert calculator, an English civil engineer named Blyth, says in a letter:

"I am conscious of an intuitive recognition of the relations of figures. For instance, in reading statements of figures in newspapers, which are often egregiously wrong, it seems to come to me intuitively that something is wrong, and when that occurs I am usually right."

In the case of at least one lightning calculator there is proof positive of the concurrent operation of two trains of thought, the one conscious, the other subconscious. This is Jedediah Buxton, who "would talk freely while doing his questions, that being no molestation or hindrance to him."

Moreover, prodigious memory power is nearly always characteristic of the lightning calculator. This of itself is evidence of unusual access to the subconscious, since it is in the subconscious that memories are stored. Most impressive of all, however, is the rapid, almost instantaneous emergence of the answers to the problems propounded by those testing the calculator's powers. It is as though the mere putting of the problem, and the mere desire to solve it, were enough to set in motion a "thinking machine" that automatically brought about the desired result. It is significant that in most cases, as in Bidder's, the calculators themselves are unable to give any satisfactory account of the methods they employ, and sometimes frankly admit that they "do not know how the answers come."

Now, this sudden irruption of ideas, this dazzling solution of problems, is characteristic not only of calculating prodigies, but also of all men of genius. They may not have—in truth, they have comparatively seldom—such a spectacular resort to the subconscious; but they assuredly have it in an astonishing measure, and to better purpose. Precisely as we find the answers to mathematical puzzles rising spontaneously in the minds of ready reckoners, so, time and again, do we find great thoughts, amounting it may be to epoch-making conceptions, forcing themselves upon men of genius, frequently at moments when they are consciously thinking of some other matter, or are not consciously exercising their minds at all. And again we have only to go to the published testimony of men of genius themselves to obtain a strong body of evidence bearing out this statement.

Many a poet of the first order, puzzling over the state of his mind during his creative moments, has declared that his works were composed as in a dream, the main ideas, sometimes even the phrases used, shaping themselves of their own accord in his consciousness. "Often it happened to me," says Goethe, "that I would repeat a song to myself and then be unable to recollect it; that sometimes I would run to my desk, and, without taking time to lay my paper straight, would, without stirring from my place, write out the poem from beginning to end, slopingly. For the same reason I always preferred to write with a pencil, on account of its marking so readily. On several occasions, indeed, the scratching and spluttering of my pen awoke me from my somnambulistic poetising and distracted me so that it suffocated a little product in its birth." (Hirsch's "Genius and Degeneration," p. 33.)

Elsewhere Goethe specifically states that his "Werther" was written "somewhat unconsciously, like a sleepwalker." And, according to Vischer, the poet Schiller, Goethe's almost equally great contemporary, complained that whenever he was consciously at work creating and constructing, his imagination was hampered and did not perform "with the same freedom as it had done when nobody was looking over its shoulder."

"It is not I who think," confesses Lamartine, "but my ideas which think for me." Dante had much the same feeling, as recorded in his famous lines, "I am so constituted that when love inspires me, I attend; and according as it speaks in me, I express myself." Voltaire, who wrote to Diderot that "in the works of genius instinct is everything," on seeing one of his own tragedies performed, exclaimed, "Was it really I who wrote that?"

"My conceptions," says Rémy de Gourmont, "rise into the field of consciousness like a flash of lightning or the flight of a bird."

"One does not work, one listens; it is as though another were speaking into one's ear," writes De Musset. Exactly similar is the statement of the composer, Hoffman:

"When I compose, I sit down to the piano, shut my eyes, and play what I hear."

From other great musicians comes equally emphatic testimony to the part played by the subconscious in the creation of their works. Mozart frankly avowed that his compositions came "involuntarily, like dreams." Among eminent composers of to-day Saint-Saens has only to listen, like Socrates, to his Dæmon; and Vincent d'Indy, writing to Dr. Paul Chabaneix (to whose "Le Subconsciente chez les Artistes, les Savants, et les Ecrivains" I am indebted for most of these French instances) relates that he "often has, on waking, a fugitive glimpse of a musical effect which—like the memory of a dream—needs a strong immediate concentration of mind to keep it from vanishing."

The situation is the same, in whatever field genius finds expression. Napoleon, by many considered the greatest military genius in the history of mankind, believed from his own experience that the fate of battles usually turned not so much on conscious planning and manœuvring as on tactics dictated by "latent thoughts" arising suddenly in the mind. "The decisive moment approached; the spark burst forth, and one was victorious." In like manner there frequently has come to scientists and inventors, with the unexpectedness of lightning out of a clear sky, the discovery of natural laws or mechanical principles of which they previously had no conscious knowledge whatever.

Everybody has heard the story of Newton, the falling apple, and the discovery of the law of gravitation; and of Galileo's invention of the pendulum, born of the thoughts springing up in his mind while idly watching the oscillations of the great bronze lamp swinging from the roof of Pisa Cathedral. Not so well known, but particularly impressive because of its revelation of the manner in which the desultory development of a train of thought in the mind of a man of genius may lead to a subconscious upsurging of the highest value, is Alfred Russel Wallace's own account of his epoch-making discovery of the scientific doctrine of the origin of species—a discovery achieved by him, in the far-off Malay Archipelago, with no knowledge that the same doctrine had even then been worked out, though not as yet made public, by Charles Darwin.

"At the time in question," Wallace relates, in his "My Life," "I was suffering from a sharp attack of intermittent fever, and every day during the cold and succeeding hot fits had to lie down for several hours, during which time I had nothing to do but to think over any subjects then particularly interesting me. One day something brought to my mind Malthus's 'Principle of Population,' which I had read about twelve years before. I thought of his clear exposition of the 'positive checks to increase'—disease, accidents, war, and famine—which keep down the population of savage races to so much lower an average than that of more civilised peoples. It then occurred to me that these causes, or their equivalents, are continually acting in the case of animals also; and as animals usually breed much more rapidly than does mankind, the destruction every year from these causes must be enormous in order to keep down the numbers of each species, since they evidently do not increase regularly from year to year, as otherwise the world would long ago have been densely crowded with those that breed most quickly.

"Vaguely thinking over the enormous and constant destruction which this implied, it occurred to me to ask the question, Why do some die and some live? And the answer was clearly, that on the whole the best fitted live. From the effects of disease the most healthy escaped; from enemies, the strongest, the swiftest, or the most cunning; from famine, the best hunters or those with the best digestion; and so on. Then it suddenly flashed on me that this self-acting process would necessarily *improve the race,* because in every generation the inferior would inevitably be killed off and the superior would remain—that is, *the fittest would survive.*

"At once I seemed to see the whole effect of this, that when changes of land and sea, or of climate, or of food-supply, or of enemies occurred—and we know that such changes have always been taking place—and considering the amount of individual variation that my experience as a collector had shown me to exist, then it followed that all the changes necessary for the adaptation of the species to the changing conditions would be brought about; and as great changes in the environment are always slow, there would be ample time for the change to be effected by the survival of the best fitted in every generation. In this way every part of an animal's organisation could be modified exactly as required, and in the very process of this modification the unmodified would die out, and thus the *definite* characters and the clear *isolation* of each new species would be explained. The more I thought about it, the more I became convinced that I had at last found the long-sought-for law of nature that solved the problem of the origin of species."

This passage, with its significant phrases, "Then it suddenly flashed on me," and "At once I seemed to see the whole effect of this," makes very clear the subconscious element in the achieving of the momentous discovery. It also emphasises another fact indispensable to a complete understanding not alone of Wallace's achievement but of the achievements of all men of genius: the fact that creative upsurgings from the subconscious would be valueless—would, indeed, be impossible of occurrence—in any but a mind rendered by conscious study, observation, and reflection, capable of appreciating their significance.

The subconscious, let me recall, is a kind of workshop where the "ego" rummages among the memory-images of its past experiences to develop trains of thought and reach definite conclusions with a minimum of effort. Obviously the results of its rummaging will depend on the material it finds to work with; in proportion as this is rich and abundant, the subconscious upsurgings will be "worth while." Obviously, too, both the richness of the material and the character and value of the subconscious upsurgings will ultimately depend on the character of the individual's interests, and the extent to which these impel him to conscious study, observation, and reflection.

Wherefore it is that all men of genius have been great workers. Even when, as has been observed in certain cases, they indulge in more or less protracted periods of idleness, they later make amends by an unusual industry; and, for that matter, their idleness often is more seeming than real, their minds being busied all the while with some baffling problem. Ardent, whole-souled absorption in the thing he has set himself to do—that, unquestionably, is a distinguishing characteristic of the man of genius. It is almost as if by instinct he labours hard to provide his subconsciousness with the data it must have in order to afford him, by way of recompense, those flashes of insight, those moments of "inspiration," that mean acknowledged leadership among his fellow-men.

I have already quoted Robert Louis Stevenson's description of what his subconscious did for him. Let me now give his account of how he toiled to provide his subconscious with its working material. Never was there a man who strove more diligently and deliberately to attain success as an author; and this even while he was a student in college, where most of those who knew him thought that his chief occupation was "killing time." As he tells us:

"All through my boyhood and youth I was known and pointed out for the pattern of an idler; and yet I was always busy on my own private end, which was to learn to write. I kept always two books in my pocket, one to read, one to write in. As I walked, my mind was busy fitting what I saw with appropriate words. When I sat by the roadside, I would either read, or a pencil and a penny version book would be in my hand, to write down the features of the scene or commemorate some halting stanzas.

"Thus I lived with words. And what I thus wrote was for no ulterior use; it was written consciously for practice. It was not so much that I wished to be an author—though I wished that, too—as that I had vowed that I would learn to write. That was a proficiency that tempted me; and I practised to acquire it, as men learn to whittle, in a wager with myself.... I worked in other ways, also; often accompanied my walks with dramatic dialogues, in which I played many parts; and often exercised myself in writing down conversations from memory.

"This was all excellent, no doubt; so were the diaries I sometimes tried to keep, but always and very speedily discarded, finding them a school of posturing and melancholy self-deception. And yet this was not the most efficient part of my training. Good though it was, it only taught me—so far as I have learned them at all—the lower and less intellectual elements of the art, the choice of the essential note and the right word; things that to a happier constitution had perhaps come by nature. And regarded as training it had one grave defect; for it set me no standard of achievement.

"So that there was, perhaps, more profit, as there was certainly more effort, in my secret labours at home. Whenever I read a book or a passage that particularly pleased me, in which a thing was said or an effect rendered with propriety, in which there was either some conspicuous force or some happy distinction in the style, I must sit down at once and set myself to ape that quality. I was unsuccessful, and I knew it; and tried again, and was again unsuccessful, and always unsuccessful; but at least in these vain bouts I got some practice in rhythm, in harmony, in construction, and the coordination of parts."

Balzac, the greatest novelist that France has ever produced, similarly exemplifies the laborious industry of the man of genius in providing his subconsciousness with material for future use, and training it to respond more fully to the demands of the upper consciousness. It was Balzac's habit to wander for days among the people, inquiring into their customs, manners, motives, and ways of thinking; and he would travel a hundred miles to get the data for a few lines of description. The result, when his genius began to show itself, after a long and painful period of incubation, was the creation of a series of works that will be read and reread as long as books are printed.

Of Dante, Boccaccio tells us that "taken by the sweetness of knowing the truth of the things concealed in Heaven, and finding no other pleasure dearer to him in life, he left all other worldly care and gave himself to this alone; and, that no part of philosophy might remain unseen by him, he plunged with acute intellect into the deepest recesses of theology, and so far succeeded in his design that, caring nothing for heat or cold, or watchings or fastings, or any other bodily discomforts, by assiduous study he came to know of the divine essence and of the other separate intelligences that the human intellect can comprehend."

Napoleon is known to have occupied his mind almost incessantly with problems of military strategy. Even at the opera he would forget the music in wrestling with such questions as, "I have ten thousand men at Strassburg, fifteen thousand at Magdeburg, twenty thousand at Würzburg. By what stages must they march so as to reach Ratisbon on three successive days?" Mozart, on the contrary, thought, lived, and moved in an atmosphere of music. He could not so much as go for a walk or play a game of billiards without humming to himself over and over again airs that he was striving to develop to his satisfaction.

"Nobody," he once declared, "takes so much pains in the study of composition as I. You could not easily name a famous master in music whom I have not industriously studied, often going through his works several times."

Schiller, even as a boy, "felt that without diligence no mastery can be won." Halley once asked Newton how he had made his marvellous discoveries in the physical realm. "By always thinking about them," was his reply. Thus the record might be continued down to the Edisons and Bergsons and Debussys of to-day.

Quite evidently, what happens is that the perpetual concentration of attention on some one problem or set of problems, not merely deposits in the subconscious an exceptional wealth of material, but also favours the emergence of the results of its manipulation of that material. Just as, in the case of the ordinary man, it is only when he is intensely interested in, say, the detection of an error in book-keeping, that he is likely to have the cause of that error made plain to him by a sudden "happy thought," or through the medium of a dream.

It may, then, be stated as a well-established fact that intense interest plus persistent effort is the prime essential to the highest success in any sphere of human activity. Of importance, also, is the fact that, as a general thing, the "set" of a man's mind, the direction which his interest most readily takes, is indicated more or less clearly in the first years of life. This is proved not only by the early lives of the world's most eminent men and women, but also by the results of careful statistical investigations into the life histories of "average" people. Especially impressive are the findings of an inquiry carried out not long ago by that well-known American psychologist, Edward L. Thorndike, and reported by him in *The Popular Science Monthly*, vol. lxxxi (1912).

Professor Thorndike submitted to one hundred third year students in Columbia College, Barnard College, and Teachers' College, New York, a list of subjects of study, including mathematics, history, literature, science, drawing, and such hand-work as carving, carpentering, gardening, etc. Each student was required to fill in a tabular blank showing the order in which the various subjects were of greatest interest to that particular student: (1) during the last three years of elementary school attendance, (2) during the high school period, and (3) at the time of the investigation. Blanks were also to be filled indicating the student's judgment as to his or her ability in each of the respective subjects during the period covered by the inquiry.

From the statistics thus gathered two things stood out clearly. No fewer than 60 per cent. of the students made returns showing that the subjects which appealed to them most strongly in their college work were the subjects that had most interested them in early life; and an even closer correspondence (65 per cent.) was shown between intensity of interest and intellectual ability. Professor Thorndike then extended his investigation to include two hundred other individuals, and obtained virtually the same results.

"These facts," it is not surprising to find him saying in comment, "unanimously witness to the importance of early interests. They are shown to be far from fickle and evanescent.... It would indeed be hard to find any feature of a human being which was a more permanent fact of his nature than his relative degree of interest in different lines of thought and action."

What this means, unquestionably, is that every parent, in planning the education of his children or in assisting them to choose a vocation, should make a real effort to gain some insight into their special interests. Not only so, but there is reason for adding that he should also endeavour to ascertain and cultivate those interests while his children are still quite young. Otherwise he is likely to find them growing to manhood and womanhood—as, under present conditions, most children do grow—with the strongest of their "worth while" interests so attenuated that really effective mental effort is next to impossible. In these circumstances—unless they chance, as Charles Darwin did, to come under the influence of a personality able to rouse their dormant powers into exceptional activity—the likelihood is that they will achieve only mediocre results, muddling along through life even when they happen to hit on vocations truly suited to them.

Are we to infer that children, at a tender age, should be encouraged to think seriously about serious subjects? Assuredly, provided the subjects be made sufficiently interesting to them. It is not without significance that a large majority of men of genius have been distinguished for their precocity; or, if not precocious in the ordinary sense of the term, they have busied themselves in childhood with mental activities allied to those for which they afterward attained eminence.

Napoleon's interest in military problems dates from his boyhood. Lord Kelvin, the foremost physicist of the nineteenth century, was making electrical machines when only nine years old, and played with them as other children play with dolls and marbles. Thomas Hobbes translated the "Medea" of Euripides into Latin iambic verse before he was fourteen. Cicero at thirteen is credited with having written a treatise on the art of oratory. Fénelon preached his first sermon when only fifteen years old. Grotius at the age of fourteen was widely known for his learning. Hallam, the famous historian, could read well before he was five, and had turned author four years later. Galileo, like Lord Kelvin, constructed mechanical toys in his childhood.

Not to accumulate instances tediously, it need only be added that, in making a survey of the biographies of a thousand eminent British men and women, the English psychologist, Havelock Ellis, found that only forty-four were specifically mentioned as not having been precocious, while nearly three hundred were mentioned as having been distinctly precocious in one sense or another. Even in the case of the forty-four, Mr. Ellis discovered, several were really as precocious as any of the three hundred, being "already absorbed in their own lines of mental activity." To this class belong, for example, Landor, Byron, and Wiseman, the last of whom is described as having been in boyhood, "dull and stupid, always reading and thinking." Nor, according to the results of Mr. Ellis's investigation, did precocity have any unfavourable effect on the health of these men and women of genius.

All similar investigations, in fact, go to show that intellectual activity makes for longevity—that those who think hardest are likely to live longest. Of one group of nearly eight hundred and fifty men of genius it was found that only two hundred and fifty died before they were sixty years old, while one hundred and thirty-one lived to be eighty or older. For another group of five hundred, an average life-span of nearly sixty-five years was found, as against a life-span of fifty-one years for all classes of people who pass the age of twenty. In the case of still another group, studied by a third investigator, an average of seventy-one years was established.

What gives these figures greater significance is the fact that in many instances the man of genius is exceptionally frail in early life. Mr. Ellis, in his statistical study, found that more than two hundred—or more than 20 per cent. of the eminent men and women included in his survey—were "congenitally of a notably feeble constitution," yet that among these were some of the longest lived. How is this to be explained? Only on the theory that the joy they felt in doing work congenial to them promoted bodily as well as mental vigour. And, in point of fact, it is to-day a commonplace among psychologists that pleasurable emotions make for increased strength, while disagreeable feelings make for weakness.

Viewed from whatever angle, therefore, "being interested" is one of the most important things in the world to every one of us. The earlier we become interested—intensely interested—in some specific field of activity, the brighter our future prospects will be.

But—this is the crucial question in the present connection—is the awaking of a lively interest, an interest so intense that it spurs to incessant endeavour in some special field, sufficient to account for the achievements of the man of genius? Granting that the man of genius depends for his results, as I have tried to show, on the extent to which he upbuilds and stimulates his subconscious powers by conscious observation and thought, must we not assume that he possesses, to begin with, an exceptional mental capacity? Or is favouring circumstance in his environment—the occurrence of events that make so profound an impression on his mind as to arouse a fervent longing for accomplishment—sufficient to explain him? In short, would it be possible, by careful education and the wise adjustment of environmental influences, so to develop any individual of normal mentality that he might achieve in his chosen life-work results usually regarded as bearing the stamp of genius?

Such, decidedly, is my belief. I base it partly on the repeated failure of investigators to demonstrate the operation of heredity in the making of the vast multitude of men of genius who, in the history of mankind, have sprung from all sorts and conditions of ancestors, rich and poor, proud and humble, wise and ignorant. Partly I base it on the many instances in which men of genius have themselves been able to trace the determination of their activities to fortunate happenings in early life. But most of all I base it on certain experiments in education undertaken by parents entirely unaware of the interrelationship between conscious thinking and subconscious "inspiration," yet intuitively believing that the sooner a child is habituated to using his mind to good purpose the more he will accomplish in later life.

IV

INTENSIVE CHILD CULTURE

The student body of Harvard University at present includes three youths whose remarkable intellectual achievements and the manner of their upbringing have given rise to much discussion in American educational circles. The oldest of these students was graduated from Tufts College at the age of fourteen, gained the degree of Ph.D. at Harvard when only eighteen, and now is continuing his studies abroad as the holder of a Harvard travelling fellowship. The youngest of the trio became a special student at Harvard before he was twelve, was graduated with honours when scarcely sixteen, and is at present engaged in post-graduate studies. The third passed the regular Harvard entrance examinations when less than fourteen, completed his college course with distinction in three years, and to-day is studying law.

What has excited controversial interest in these youths is not so much their precocity, striking though that is, as the fact that in each case they have been educated along novel lines from their earliest childhood. Their fathers, who have worked independently of one another, assert, indeed, that their unusual mental development is not due to any exceptional talent, but is the result of the peculiar home training they have received; the implication being that a similar development is possible to every normal child if reared in the same way. Besides which, the fathers contend that the prevailing method of giving children little or no formal education until they are old enough to go to school is fundamentally wrong; that the home is the proper place in which to begin a child's education, and that the proper time to begin is with the first dawning of the child's ability and desire to use his reasoning powers. Or, as one of them has recently declared:

"In the large majority of children the beginning of education should be between the second and third year. It is at that time that the child begins to form his interests. It is at that critical period that we have to seize the opportunity to guide the child's formative energies in the right channels. To delay is a mistake and a wrong to the child. We can at that early period awaken a love of knowledge which will persist through life. The child will as eagerly play in the game of knowledge as he now spends the most of his energies in meaningless games and objectless, silly sports." (Boris Sidis's "Philistine and Genius," pp. 67–68.)

Some few educators in this country have already tentatively approved the new ideas in child-training as exemplified by the methods pursued and the results obtained in the case of these youthful Harvard students. For the most part, however, their promulgation has been greeted skeptically, even with caustic criticism. On the one hand, it is alleged that the parents cannot positively prove that the achievements of their boys are not the result of inherited gifts rather than the special education given them; and, on the other hand, the position is taken that, assuming the correctness of their fathers' contention in this respect, it is by no means evident that such training is desirable.

In the words of one critic, to begin the education of a child at two or three is to rob that child of his childhood. The training in question is described as a "forcing" system, much talk is heard of "mind strain," and the prediction is freely made that the ultimate outcome can only be to drive children thus educated into an asylum for the insane, or into an early grave.

My own belief is that the critics are wrong. I have long been acquainted with all three of these students, and in one case have had opportunity to observe rather closely the process of mental and physical development for upward of eight years. All three are sturdy, strong young fellows; if anything above the average for their years in stature and weight. Time alone, of course, can tell whether they will live to a good old age. But if they should die or become insane, I am satisfied that neither misfortune could justly be attributed to their parents' educational methods. On the contrary, the principles underlying these methods seem to me for the most part so beneficial that I believe the time will come when they will be quite generally adopted.

Decidedly, though, I should not express myself with such assurance were it not for the fact that these same principles have long ago been put to the test and impressively vindicated. I wonder if the name of James Thomson of Annaghmore has ever been heard by those who have so hastily condemned the parents of the three Harvard students? Doubtless not, else they would surely have moderated their denunciations.

Thomson, who was born in the year 1786, the son of a Scotch-Irish farmer, was pre-eminently a "self-made" man. Seemingly doomed to the obscure existence of an ordinary farm-labourer, he had emancipated himself by dint of an extraordinary energy. With but slight aid he contrived, while a mere child, to teach himself to read, write, and cipher. In the fields, and by candle-light in his farm home, at every opportunity, he studied little text-books that were to him the most fascinating things in the world because they gave him knowledge. He was determined to become an educated man, and continually he urged his father to let him go to school.

To school eventually he went, in the neighbouring village of Ballykine, and there, as in his childhood, he found his greatest delight in the study of mathematics. He must, he told himself, know more about this great science; he must know everything that could be learned about it. Also, being of a religious turn of mind, he planned to fit himself to become a clergyman. Obviously, whether to learn higher mathematics, or to qualify for the ministry, it was necessary to go to college. And to college he did go; but, so difficult were his circumstances, not until he was a man full-grown.

From 1810 to 1814—that is, from the age of twenty-four to twenty-eight—he spent six months of every year at the University of Glasgow. The other six months he spent earning his living. Finally he received the coveted M.A. degree, and having in the meantime become more enamoured of mathematics than of a clerical career, he accepted appointment to the teaching staff of an academy in Belfast, where, married to a sweetheart of his Glasgow days, he soon entered upon the additional task of bringing up a family.

It is at this point that he becomes of special interest to us. For, looking back at the stupendous obstacles he himself had had to overcome in gaining an education, he resolved to do everything in his power to make the road to learning easy for his children.

To do this, it seemed to him, the proper course to pursue was to begin their education as soon as they showed an intelligent interest in the world about them. For, he argued, quite in the manner of the fathers of the three Harvard students of to-day, it is because the education of children begins too late that they find it hard to learn, and strain their minds in the attainment of knowledge. Let a child get accustomed to using his mind to good purpose in early childhood, and study will never be a tax on him but a perpetual joy. This, thought he, is the way all children should be brought up.

And, with the faithful co-operation of his wife, this was the way James Thomson brought up his own children. He taught them, boys and girls, to spell and to read almost as soon as they could speak. He taught them mathematics, history, geography, and the elements of natural science. One of the busiest of men—for he was a writer of mathematical textbooks as well as a classroom instructor—he made great sacrifices for the sake of their education. He would even get up at four in the morning to work on his text-books and to prepare his lectures, so as to be sure of having freedom to instruct his little ones during the day. Especially he made it a point to fertilise their minds, to whet their interest in worth while things, in the course of table-talk and when out walking with them.

"When spring came," one of his daughters, Mrs. Elizabeth King, has recalled in a delightful volume of family reminiscences, "our father generally took a walk with us in the early morning before breakfast, and he used to invent interesting topics of conversation, which were carried on through successive mornings. Two of us held his hands and two walked quite near, but the places of honour were shared alternately by the four. I remember all being intensely interested in a series of talks on the progress of civilisation, in which every one, even little Willie, suggested ideas, and took part in the conversation.

"We also in these walks made imaginary voyages of discovery, full of adventure, calling at various ports, and sailing up rivers to obtain the products of the countries we visited, and become acquainted with the inhabitants. We explored the icy regions of the north, the burning deserts of Africa and Arabia, and the fragrant forests of Ceylon. There was no end to our travels and the wonders we saw when we walked with our father. Sometimes we transported ourselves to ancient days, and sailed with the Argonauts in search of the golden fleece, or accompanied the Greeks to Troy to recover the beautiful Helen, or joined Ulysses in his protracted wanderings. Our father always led the talk, but we all assisted."

His two older sons, James and William, were the special objects of his care, particularly after their mother's death, which occurred when James was eight and William six. After this sad event he lived more than ever with these two boys, giving up part of his bedroom to them, and diligently drilling them in the rudiments of an all-round education. When, in 1832, he was appointed professor of mathematics at his old university, he continued their home training, and in addition obtained permission for them to attend his university lectures and the lectures of some other professors.

Two years later, James being then twelve and William ten, they were admitted as full-fledged undergraduates. And, precocious though they were, they also were healthy, vigorous, active boys, full of fun and eager to romp and play. Like other boys they delighted in games and toys, with the sole difference that in many instances their toys were scientific instruments. Thus, they made with their own hands little electrical machines with which to give harmless and laughter-provoking shocks to their friends.

In a word, all who knew them liked them—and marvelled at them. There was abundant cause for marvel. Not only did they keep up with their studies with ease, but in more than one department of knowledge they outdid their classmates, some of whom were well into their twenties. The following excerpt from "The Book of the Jubilee" gives a vivid idea of the scholastic achievements of these two remarkable boys in the first years of their life at Glasgow University:

"At the end of his first winter's work William Thomson carried off two prizes in the Humanity Class; this before he was eleven. In the next session we follow him to the classes of Natural History and Greek—we wonder what the present occupants of these chairs would say to a stripling under twelve who presented himself at their lectures—and his name figures in both prize-lists.

"Sympathy is not lacking for the hard-worked school-boy of to-day; but what would the child of twelve think of the holiday task of translating Lucian's 'Dialogues of the Gods,' with full parsing of the first three dialogues! This is the piece of work for which William Thomson, Glasgow College, receives a prize in May, 1836.

"Next session we find the two brothers together in the Junior Mathematical Class, of the Junior Division of which they are first and second prize-men. They appear again at the head of the list for the Monthly Voluntary Examinations on the work of the class and its applications. Proceeding to the Senior Mathematical Class in 1837–38, they again stand at the top, nor have they failed to present themselves for the Voluntary Examinations. William is not satisfied with this class, but in addition receives the second prize in the Junior Division of Professor Robert Buchanan's Logic Class."

And, continuing to win laurels, at the close of the next session they took the first and second places as prize-men in natural philosophy, while William the following year gained the class prize in astronomy, and was awarded a university medal for an essay, "On the Figure of the Earth," the manuscript of which, a carefully bound volume of eighty-five pages, is still in existence. He was then not sixteen years old.

Of course there were not lacking wiseacres who dolefully predicted all manner of unpleasant things for these "unhappy victims of a father's folly," who must inevitably fade into an early grave. But the father only smiled serenely, confident that the future would vindicate his educational innovation. And, of a surety, the future did. For James Thomson, the older of the two, living to the age of seventy, left behind him the reputation of one of England's leading authorities on engineering; while William, who did not die until he was eighty-three, became even more famous, winning, as Lord Kelvin of Largs, a place in the annals of science fairly comparable with that held by the immortal Newton.

A similar process of intensive child culture was carried out, with similarly happy results, in the case of John Stuart Mill, whose father modelled his whole upbringing in accordance with the theory that the mind, like the body, grows with exercise, and that the sooner the process of exercising and training it begins, the better the child's prospects for a worthy and efficient manhood. Like James Thomson the elder Mill was an exceedingly busy man, but this did not prevent him from making the intellectual development of his son a matter of patient, personal attention. Almost as soon as the little John could talk, his formal education began, and throughout his childhood was continued along lines that have provoked indignant comment in many quarters.

"I have no remembrance," he tells us, in his interesting "Autobiography," "of the time when I began to learn Greek. I have been told that it was when I was three years old. My earliest recollection on the subject is that of committing to memory what my father termed vocables, being lists of common Greek words, with their signification in English, which he wrote out for me on cards. Of grammar, until some years later, I learned no more than the inflexions of the nouns and verbs, but after a course of vocables, proceeded at once to translation; and I faintly remember going through 'Æsop's Fables,' the first Greek book which I read. The 'Anabasis,' which I remember better, was the second. I learned no Latin until my eighth year.

"At that time I had read, under my father's tuition, a number of Greek prose authors, among whom I remember the whole of Herodotus, and of Xenophon's 'Cyropaedia' and 'Memorials of Socrates'; some of the lives of the philosophers by Diogenes Laertius; part of Lucian; and 'Isocrates ad Demonicum' and 'Ad Nicoclem.'... What he himself was willing to undergo for the sake of my instruction, may be judged from the fact that I went through the whole process of preparing my Greek lessons in the same room and at the same table at which he was writing; and as in those days Greek and English lexicons were not, and I could make no more use of a Greek and Latin lexicon than could be made without having yet begun to learn Latin, I was forced to have recourse to him for the meaning of every word which I did not know. This incessant interruption he, one of the most impatient of men, submitted to, and wrote under that interruption several volumes of his history and all else that he had to write during those years.

"The only thing besides Greek that I learned as a lesson in this part of my childhood was arithmetic; this also my father taught me. It was the task of the evenings, and I well remember its disagreeableness. But the lessons were only a part of the daily instruction I received. Much of it consisted in the books I read by myself, and my father's discourses to me, chiefly during our walks.

"From 1810 to 1813 (that is, from Mill's fourth to eighth year) we were living in Kensington Green, then an almost rustic neighbourhood. My father's health required considerable and constant exercise, and he walked habitually before breakfast, generally in the green lanes toward Hornsey. In these walks I always accompanied him, and with my earliest recollections of green fields and wild-flowers, is mingled that of the account I gave him daily of what I had read the day before. To the best of my remembrance, this was a voluntary rather than a prescribed exercise. I made notes on slips of paper while reading, and from these in the morning walks I told the story to him....

"In these frequent talks about the books I read, he used, as opportunity offered, to give me explanations and ideas respecting civilisation, government, morality, mental cultivation, which he required me afterward to restate to him in my own words.... He was fond of putting into my hands books which exhibited men of energy and resource in unusual circumstances, struggling against difficulties and overcoming them: of such works I remember Beaver's 'African Memoranda,' and Collins's 'Account of the First Settlement of New South Wales.'... Of children's books, any more than of playthings, I had scarcely any, except an occasional gift from a relation or acquaintance: among those I had, 'Robinson Crusoe' was preeminent, and continued to delight me through all my boyhood.

"It was no part, however, of my father's system to exclude books of amusement, though he allowed them very sparingly. Of such books he possessed at that time next to none, but he borrowed several for me; those which I remember are the 'Arabian Nights,' Cazotte's 'Arabian Tales,' 'Don Quixote,' Miss Edgeworth's 'Popular Tales,' and a book of some reputation in its day, Brooke's 'Fool of Quality.'"

In one respect, it must be conceded, Mill's early education was deficient—it depended altogether too much on the knowledge to be gained from books, and not enough on direct study of the laws and beauties of Nature. But against this stands the unquestionable fact that it did establish in him lifelong habits of industry and thoroughness, and an abiding joy in intellectual achievement; and, more important, it had the happy result of habituating him to regard himself as consecrated to a life of labour for the public good. As to the "wrong" done to Mill by "robbing him of the joys of childhood," one of his biographers, Professor William Minto, justly observes:

"Much pity has been expressed over the dreary, cheerless existence that the child must have led, cut off from all boyish amusements and companionship, working day after day on his father's treadmill; but a childhood and boyhood spent in the enlargement of knowledge, with the continual satisfaction of difficulties conquered, buoyed up by day-dreams of emulating the greatest of human benefactors, need not have been an unhappy childhood, and Mill expressly says that his was not unhappy. It seems unhappy only when we compare it with the desires of childhood left more to itself, and when we decline to imagine its peculiar enjoyments and aspirations. Mill complains that his father often required more than could be reasonably expected of him, but his tasks were not so severe as to prevent him from growing up a healthy, hardy, and high-spirited boy, though he was not constitutionally robust, and his tastes and pursuits were so different from those of other boys of the same age."

Mill was never a college student, and was for the most part self-educated after his sixteenth year. But had he been sent to college at an early age, as his home training amply warranted, there is every reason to think he would have acquitted himself as brilliantly as did the Thomson boys, and as did Karl Witte, another noteworthy example of the possibilities open to all parents. Indeed, Witte's case is in some respects the most interesting and instructive on record. For one thing his father has left a minutely detailed account of the methods employed in his education; and there is ground to suspect that at the outset of life Karl Witte was below rather than above the average in mentality.

Born in July, 1800, in the German village of Lochau, near Halle, he was the son of a country clergyman, likewise named Karl Witte, who had long been regarded as somewhat "eccentric." In especial the elder Witte was known to hold "peculiar" views on education. It was his firm belief, just as it was the belief of James Thomson and James Mill, that only by beginning the educational process in infancy could one make sure of developing children into really rational men and women. Looking at the world about him, and noting the extent to which people wasted their lives in hopeless inefficiency and reckless dissipation, he said to himself, in effect:

"These poor people do not reason, do not use their God-given intellects. If they did they would conduct themselves altogether differently. The trouble must be that they have not been educated aright. They have not been taught how to think, and what to think about. They have been started wrong in life. The schools and universities are to blame, but far more their parents are to blame. If love of the good, the beautiful, and the true had been implanted in them in youth, if they had been trained from the first in the proper use of their minds, they would not now be living so foolishly."

Holding these views, Pastor Witte promised himself that if God blessed him with children he would make their education his special care. His first child, however, died in early infancy. Then came Karl, at birth so unprepossessing and "stupid" in appearance that his father wondered in what way he had offended God that he should be afflicted with a witless child. The neighbours, sympathising, held out what hopes they could, but secretly agreed that Pastor Witte's boy was undoubtedly an idiot.

Thus matters stood until one day the father fancied that he detected in the child signs of intelligence. There and then he set about "making a man of him," as he expressed it. He began, even before Karl could speak, by naming to him different parts of the human body, objects in his bedroom, etc. Later, as soon as the child was old enough to toddle about, he gradually broadened the horizon of his knowledge, taking him for walks through the streets and fields of Lochau, and calling his attention to all sorts of interesting things. Encouraging him to ask questions he went in his replies as fully as possible into the essential details of the subject under discussion. Above all, he avoided giving superficial answers, for it was his great aim to impress on Karl the importance of reasoning closely, of appreciating relationships and dissimilarities. If the child asked him something to which he could not respond intelligently, he frankly confessed his ignorance, but suggested that by working together they might obtain a satisfactory answer.

Also, in his daily walks and conversations with his son, "baby talk" had no place. It was part of Pastor Witte's theory, as it is part of Doctor Berle's to-day, that this mode of addressing children, however it may appeal to the sentimental side of fathers and mothers, is intellectually enervating to their little ones. The child who would think correctly, he argued, must be taught to speak correctly.

For this reason he not only drilled Karl in the correct pronunciation and use of words, but insisted that all who talked with the child should be careful how they spoke to him. Besides which, with an intuitive appreciation of the formative value of even the seemingly most trivial details of the home environment, he arranged the household furnishings so that they too, by the subtle influence of suggestion, should contribute powerfully to Karl's development. As he tells us in his own account, of which an abridged translation into English has recently been made by Professor Leo Wiener, of Harvard University:[1]

"I tolerated as far as possible nothing in my house, yard, garden, etc., that was not tasteful, especially nothing that did not harmonise with its surroundings. If anything was not harmonious, I was uneasy about it until it was removed. All my rooms were papered with wall-paper of one colour, the fields being surrounded by pleasing borders. In every room there was but little furniture, but such as there was, was carefully selected. On all the walls hung paintings or etchings, but none of these was tastelessly glaring in colours, or represented an unpleasant subject. Our yard and garden were in bloom from earliest Spring to very late in the Fall. Snowbells and crocuses started the procession, and winter asters were crushed only by the snow or a severe frost. We ourselves were always dressed cleanly but simply."

At first, it must be said, Karl's mother had scant sympathy with her husband's enthusiasm. She felt that he was mistaken, that the child was "too stupid" to be educated, and that nothing would come of the pains taken with him. This was the general belief of the neighbourhood, but it gave place to a feeling of astonished incredulity upon the discovery that in reality the youngster was making extraordinary progress, and was displaying not only intelligence but a love of knowledge rarely seen in boys of any age. Before he was six all who talked with him were amazed at the proofs he gave of the great extent to which he had profited from his early training.

Most impressive was the accuracy and fulness of the information he even then possessed regarding a variety of subjects, and his linguistic proficiency. His study of foreign languages began with French, while he still was very young, and was conducted in a novel way, his father giving him French translations of books with which he was already familiar in German, and telling him to read them for a certain time each day. No attempt was made to teach him the grammar of the language as it is commonly taught in the schools, his father's belief being that the boy could best pick up the grammar for himself in the course of his reading, and that he would be able to master the French translations with comparatively little trouble by reason of his previous training in the art of observation, analysis, and synthesis. This expectation was realised so fully that, according to his father's statement, Karl within a year was reading French with ease.

Meantime he had begun the study of Italian, and from Italian passed to Latin. Chance played some part in introducing him to this language. His father had taken him to a concert in Leipzig, and during an intermission handed him the libretto. He looked at it casually, then with some intentness, and exclaimed:

"Why, father, this is not French, nor is it Italian. It must be Latin!"

"Let it be what it may," said Witte, "if only you can make out what it means. Try at least."

The boy, already grounded in two languages derived from Latin, puzzled out the meaning with considerable success, and declared enthusiastically:

"Father, if Latin is such an easy language as this, I should like to learn it."

English came next, and then the study of Greek, a language regarding which the boy's curiosity was whetted by tales from Homer and Xenophon told to him by his father. Again the process was chiefly one of self-education, the father answering—when he could—the questions put to him by Karl, but always insisting to the latter that the proper way to learn anything is to overcome its difficulties for oneself. He was now studying and reading French, Italian, Latin, English, and Greek, in all of which he made such progress that, we are told, by the time he was nine he had read Homer, Plutarch, Virgil, Cicero, Fénelon, Florian, and Metastasio in the original, besides Schiller and other classical German writers.

Naturally the fame of the boy spread abroad, and with its spreading his father came in for some sharp criticism. Formerly he had been laughed at as a man who was essaying the impossible in striving to impart intelligence to a mentally subnormal child. Now that he had succeeded so well in his undertaking people asserted that he was fanatically endeavouring to convert the child into a weird thinking machine, and endangering his health and sanity. Precisely the same objections, in short, were raised to his educational experiment that were later raised in the case of the Thomson boys and John Stuart Mill, and that have recently been raised against the educational methods of the fathers of the three youths now in Harvard.

All kinds of absurd stories were circulated regarding Karl. He was pictured quite generally as a pale, anæmic, puny, goggle-eyed "freak," who had missed the delights of childhood and was vastly to be pitied. In reality, he was a happy, joyous youngster, who got as much "fun" out of life as any boy could. This is the unanimous testimony of those who "investigated" the lad for themselves. Thus the archæologist Heyne, in a statement to his friend the famous philosopher and poet Wieland, frankly admitted:

"I allowed myself to be persuaded to examine young Witte, in order to be able to form my own opinion of him. I found the boy in body and mind happy and hale to a greater degree than I had expected. I found, in testing him with Homer and Virgil, that he had sufficient knowledge of words and things to translate readily and strike the right meaning, and that, without exact grammatical and lingual knowledge, he was able to guess correctly the meaning of a passage from its context. What was most remarkable to me was that he read with understanding, feeling, and effect.

"Otherwise I found in him no preponderating faculty. Memory, imagination, reasoning, were about in equilibrium. In other matters besides those that had been inculcated by education, I found him a happy, lusty boy, not even averse from mischief, which was to me a quieting thing."

At the same time that he was thus instructing Karl in languages and literature, Witte sought to awaken in him a love of art and science. Neither artist nor scientist himself, he none the less believed that if he could only interest his son sufficiently in artistic and scientific subjects, he would study them enthusiastically. To this end he adopted a plan which might well be imitated by all parents.

Whenever he went to Halle, Leipzig, or any other German city, he took Karl with him, and together they visited art galleries, natural history museums, zoölogical and botanical gardens, and manufacturing establishments. Not for a moment, however, did he hint to the boy that he was doing this for educational purposes. When, for example, they visited a factory, he did not say, "I have brought you here to give you a lesson in mechanics." He allowed the boy to think that he simply wished to entertain him; and in this way, without Karl's suspecting it, he was able to impart to him much elementary instruction in zoölogy, botany, physics, chemistry, etc.

Similarly he taught Karl geography by the pleasing device of first taking him, on a clear day, to the top of a high tower that happened to be in Lochau, and asking him to mark on a piece of paper, brought to the tower for that purpose, the position of the different villages visible in the surrounding country. This first trip was followed by others, in which the boy expanded and corrected the markings on his paper, putting in rivers, lakes, and forests. Witte then bought for him a set of maps showing, in succession, the part of Germany in which he lived, all Germany, Europe, and the other continents. These father and son studied together, not as a study, but as a game, in which the boy took part with the greatest enthusiasm.

"I never acted," Witte himself has declared, "as though he had to learn these things. He would have been surprised if told that he had been studying geography, physics, chemistry. I avoided the mention of such terms, so as not to frighten him, and in order not to make him vain."

Not to make him vain! Be sure, indeed, that Pastor Witte, while promoting his son's mental development, would not forget to ground him in moral principles. He was not, let it be clearly understood, striving to make an intellectual "prodigy" of his son; he was aiming only to make him a man in the truest sense, strong physically and morally as well as mentally. If he believed that the boy's reasoning powers could not be properly developed unless he were trained from infancy in the principles of sound reasoning, he was quite as firmly convinced that the process of moral education should likewise begin at the earliest possible moment. To this end, believing as he did in the importance of early environmental influences and of parental example, he endeavoured to secure for his son wholly ennobling surroundings.

He even laid down rules to be observed by the maid-of-all-work, a simple but good-hearted peasant girl, in her dealings with the child. The whole family life was regulated with a view to "suggesting" to the little Karl ideas which, sinking into the subconscious region of his mind, would tend to affect favourably his moral outlook and exercise a lasting influence on his conduct. In their relations with all who visited their home—as with each other, with Karl himself, and with the little serving-maid—both Pastor Witte and his wife were unfailingly courteous, considerate, and sympathetic. Over and above all this, they set him a constant example in diligence, of that earnest activity which is itself a powerful factor in moral discipline.

Important also is it to note that in their daily walks and talks together, Karl's father took good care to cultivate in him the gift of imagination, which means so much to the moral as well as the mental growth of man. When they went hand in hand across the fields of Lochau, it was not only in rudiments of science that Witte instructed his son; he deftly awakened in him an appreciation of the sublimity and beauty in the workings of Nature. When he narrated to him stories from history, it was not merely to interest him in the study of history; the emphasis was on some moral trait exemplified by the particular story. In familiarising him with the life of Lochau itself, in introducing him to its shops and cottage-homes, the effort was tactfully made to awaken and broaden his sympathies. Always it was one of Witte's chief objects to keep his son as free as possible from anything that might make for harshness, narrowness, and intolerance in later years.

Even when Karl was not more than three or four years old, his father did not deem it too early to attempt by rebuke and admonition to instil into him the idea that he ought to guard his tongue closely to avoid hurting the feelings of other people. All children, as is well known, are inclined to "speak out in meeting," and frequently their "cute" comments, which many parents applaud as evidences of keen observational power, convey a sting to the person commented on. So soon as this universal trait of childhood appeared in little Karl his father set about suppressing it, and at the same time sought to utilise it as an aid in his moral education. The occasion arose following a thoughtless remark by the child regarding some slight eccentricity in the behaviour of a certain Herr N., a friend of the family. When father and son were alone, the former asked:

"Why did you speak of Herr N. as you did?"

"Because what I said was true."

"I grant that. It was true—it was, indeed, very true. But that is no reason you should have said it. It was neither good nor kind of you. Did you not see how disturbed he became? He would say nothing back, perhaps because of the love he bears for us. But it pained him very much that a child should say anything so unpleasant to him. If he is unhappy to-day, the fault is yours."

Witte tells us that it was not long before Karl acquired the excellent habit of "putting himself in the other fellow's place" before uttering censorious judgments. Similarly, and with equal success, his father endeavoured to broaden his sympathies so as to include the brute creation. It happened one day, when Karl was about three years old, that there were at his home a number of guests, who made much of the child, naturally to his great delight. While they were talking to him the family dog came into the room, and Karl, as any child might, playfully caught it by the tail and drew it to him. As he did so, his father, putting out his hand, caught Karl himself by his long hair and pulled it exactly as he was pulling the tail of the dog. Karl turned, saw his father's indignant look, blushed crimson, and released the dog.

At once his father released him, and demanded:

"How did you like that?"

"Not at all," was the embarrassed answer.

"Well, then, do you think the dog liked it? Now go out to the yard."

"I sent him out," Witte says, "not only as a punishment, but because I saw that some of my guests were about to open their lips to take his part and to blame me—in his presence!—for my treatment of him. But one of them, speaking suddenly, said:

"'God bless you, dear friend. If Karl, as I believe he is certain to do, shall grow to be a good man, he will thank you heartily for this lesson. I wish to Heaven we thus and always handled our children. Then they would be sure to learn to treat animals kindly, and by so much the more to treat their fellow-men kindly!"

And Witte adds, dryly:

"After this, none of those present thought it well to say anything in criticism of me."

He had, in fact, taken precisely the course best calculated to impress on Karl the vitally important principle of kindness to all living creatures. For he had brought this principle home to him in a way the child's mind could readily grasp, and without unnecessary harshness and "nagging," which, after all, only arouse those contrariant ideas that it should be the great aim of education to suppress. And it was thus that Witte and his wife always acted in the upbringing of their boy through the critical formative period of early childhood. The moment any undesirable characteristic made its appearance they hastened to awaken in him a sense of its extreme undesirability by words and conduct that appealed forcefully both to his understanding and to his emotions.

Particularly did they appeal—and here is a point deserving of special emphasis—to his sense of filial love. That they were able to make their appeal unfailingly successful, that the child always found in it a compelling motive for good behaviour, was due to the fact that their whole attitude toward him made him realise that he was an object of devoted, though not over-indulgent, love on their part. Never rebuked without a sufficient cause, and always more in sorrow than in anger; given a free hand in all things except those injurious or detrimental to him; made a companion and a playmate by both parents—he soon perceived, as any child would, that they had nothing more warmly at heart than his best interests and his happiness. Loved as he was, he gave out abundant love in return, and the great ambition of his childhood became a passionate desire to please his father and mother.

Hence it was that Witte, in carrying out his policy of early intellectual training, found no more potent spur to incite his boy to study the subjects given him than the simple statement, "You know, dear Karl, you must learn all you can, so that you will be able to care for your mother and me when we are old and feeble." Hence, too, the child acquired habits of obedience, self-control, and truthfulness, largely because of his anxiety not to bring pain to his parents. They, however, it is to be noted, were careful to discipline him firmly if he did commit a fault, but always in a way that caused him to appreciate the reasonableness of the punishment inflicted on him.

Such was the manner of Karl Witte's education up to the age of nine. By that time he had learned so much, and was so well trained in the use of his mental powers, that his father decided to send him to college. At nine and a half, to the amazement of all Germany, he entered the University of Leipzig. There, as at the universities of Göttingen, Giessen, and Heidelberg, where he also prosecuted his studies, his career was brilliant in the extreme. No subject—and he applied himself to many subjects—seemed beyond his powers. In 1814, before he had passed his fourteenth birthday, he was granted the degree of Ph.D. for a thesis on the "Conchoid of Nicomedes," a curve of the fourth degree. Two years later he was made a Doctor of Laws, and appointed to the teaching staff of the University of Berlin.

Before beginning to teach, however, it was thought best for him to spend some time in foreign travel, which he was enabled to do, thanks to the generosity of no less a personage than the King of Prussia, who had been following his university career with lively interest. Abroad, therefore, Karl Witte went, chiefly to study law, the teaching of which he had definitely selected as his profession. But toward the close of 1818 an incident occurred which, while it did not turn him from law, opened up to him another field of intellectual activity, and the one in which he ultimately won his greatest fame.

While sojourning in Florence he chanced to make the acquaintance of a talented woman who, discussing with him the masters of Italian literature, half in jest and half in earnest warned him not to attempt to read Dante, whom he could never hope to "understand." Naturally this roused his curiosity, and he promptly bought an elaborate edition of the "Divine Comedy." Reading this through, he then read what the commentators had to say about it, and was shocked at what he considered the inadequacy and positive error of their views. "Some day," said he to himself, "I will certainly make an effort to promote a better appreciation of Dante." This resolution he carried into effect five years later by the publication, in Germany, of one of the most important literary essays of the nineteenth century. It was entitled "On Misunderstanding Dante," and concerning it a modern authority on the study of Dante, Philip H. Wicksteed, declares:

"If the history of the revival of interest in Dante which has characterised this century shall ever be written, Karl Witte will be the chief hero of the tale. He was little more than a boy when, in 1823, he entered the lists against existing Dante scholars, all and sundry, demonstrated that there was not one of them that knew his trade, and announced his readiness to teach it to them. The amazing thing is that he fully accomplished his vaunt. His essay exercised a growing influence in Germany, and then in Europe; and after five-and-forty years of indefatigable and fruitful toil he was able to look back upon his youthful attempt as containing the germ of all his subsequent work on Dante. But now, instead of the audacious young heretic and revolutionist, he was the acknowledged master of the most prominent Dante scholars in Germany, Switzerland, Italy, England, and America."

In fact, from the time of the publication of this preliminary paper, almost to the time of his death, Dante essays, translations, commentaries, came from the pen of Karl Witte, to delight an ever-widening circle of Dante scholars, and incidentally to promote the study of Italian history. To understand Dante, Witte iterated and reiterated, it is absolutely necessary to have a knowledge of mediæval Italy. Especially must one study the religious preoccupation of the age, as seen in the rise of Saint Francis and Saint Dominic, the Thomist reconstitution of theology and the contemporary consolidation of the hierarchy, and the attitude of the period toward the Albigenses and other heretics. This knowledge one must gain if he would fully appreciate the true significance of the "Divine Comedy" as the portrayal of man given over to sin and prevented by his lusts from recovering the path to virtue, till the Christian religion teaches him, by the light of understanding, to recognise sin and free himself from it, and then offers to his transported vision the divine revelation of the secret and bliss of Heaven.

Yet all the while the propagation of his views on Dante and the fostering of a love for Dante were but an avocation with Karl Witte. His vocation, his life-work, was the teaching of the principles of law, both in the class-room and by the pen. It was in 1821, soon after his return from Italy, that he was established as lecturer on jurisprudence at the University of Breslau, being appointed to a full professorship two years later, and transferred to Halle in 1834. There he passed the remainder of his long and distinguished life, which did not terminate until March 6, 1883, when he passed away sincerely mourned as "a devout Christian and elder of the church, a scholar overwhelmed with honours and distinctions, a tender husband and father."

Thus the "forcing" process to which his father had subjected him did not in the least hurt Karl Witte. It is one which any conscientious and intelligent parent may make use of for his own children if he so desires. And, to my way of thinking, children reared in this way will have a far better chance for success and happiness in after years than would otherwise be theirs.

V

THE PROBLEM OF LAZINESS

From what has already been said, it is evident that there are at least three fundamental principles to be observed by all parents who would give their children a good start in life. Care must be taken to set the little ones a really good parental example; they must be surrounded from the dawn of consciousness by a favourable environment; and the effort should be made by direct instruction to develop in them habits of right thinking and acting before wrong habits have time to get formed. To these three principles a fourth must now be added: the exercise of constant vigilance to detect and correct any physical disabilities, no matter how trivial they may seem to be.

As was noted when discussing the case of the boy who "goes wrong," even comparatively slight physical defects, by causing neural stress, may contribute directly to the making of the juvenile delinquent. So, too, mental development may be hampered by unfavourable conditions of bodily health. This, of course, has long been recognised in a general way. But in essential details it still is a fact far too little appreciated by the majority of parents. Nay, it is ignored or misunderstood even by some scientific students of the nature of man, as is shown, for example, by the varying views held to-day regarding that widespread human frailty, laziness.

Only a short time ago, looking through some scientific works bearing on a complicated educational problem, I was greatly struck by two pronouncements concerning laziness. On the one hand I found an eminent physiologist declaring unreservedly, "The love of work and activity is an acquired characteristic rather than a natural one; for the human tendency is toward the line of least effort." And opposed to this another authority asserted with equal emphasis, "There never was a child born into this world who was born into it lazy."

To reconcile these statements is a manifest impossibility. Yet it is certain that each of them finds in facts of everyday observation a strong body of evidence to support it. The average child of tender years, as every parent knows, is supremely active and energetic. He is always in motion, always busying himself about something, his mind alert and inquiring, his hands ceaselessly occupied in testing, exploring, putting together, and taking to pieces. Left to himself, he often will display an amazing tenacity of purpose and vigour of performance.

Of one child, less than a year old, a close observer has recorded, "He would over and over again seem to be trying to solve the problem of the hinge to his nursery door, patiently and with riveted attention opening and shutting the door. Day after day saw him at his self-appointed task." Another, fourteen months old, while playing with a tin can, was seen to put the cover on and off "not less than seventy-nine times without stopping for a moment." The incessant questioning with which children bombard their parents is another impressive indication of their exuberant, irrepressible activity and energy. But, for that matter, the whole life of the average child goes to corroborate the dictum that the people of this world come into it free from the taint of laziness.

When, however, we look at the same child grown to manhood, or even a few years removed from early youth, more often than not his behaviour seems to bear out the contrary view that man is naturally lazy and acquires love of work, if at all, only under strong compulsion. "To get results from my boys, to induce them to apply themselves to their books and their studies," many a despairing school-teacher has lamented, "I have to be forever watching and driving them." In college, office, factory, workshop, and store, one hears the same complaint. There is perpetual waste of time, dawdling, loitering, gossiping—a seeming passion for the ways of slothful ease and aversion from sustained endeavour. To a large extent, too, the history even of those who have won distinction as leaders of thought and action seemingly justifies the doctrine that mankind is naturally prone to idleness rather than to productive activity, and that any tendency in the latter direction is invariably a characteristic acquired in the course of individual development.

Thus Charles Darwin, world-famous for his splendid contributions to the advance of science, was so lazy in boyhood that his father predicted he would turn out a ne'er-do-well and a disgrace to the family. His great contemporary, Sir Charles Lyell, similarly had as a boy a profound dislike for work of any sort. Heinrich Heine, on his own confession, idled away his time in school, and was "horribly bored" by the instruction given him at Göttingen. According to an American psychologist, Edgar James Swift, who has made an extensive study of the boyhood of great men, Wordsworth up to the age of seventeen was so lazy as to be "wholly incapable of continued application to prescribed work." Of Patrick Henry it is recorded by an early biographer that in boyhood "he was too idle to gain any solid advantage from the opportunities which were thrown in his way." And, after his schooling was done, indolence caused him to fail dismally in several business ventures before he took up the study of law.

When James Russell Lowell was a boy his relatives were greatly distressed by his laziness, and he was suspended by the authorities of Harvard University "on account of continual neglect of his college duties." A boyhood friend who had unusual facilities for observation is credited with having repeatedly declared that "there never was so idle a dog as young Humphry," afterward Sir Humphry Davy of scientific renown. "My master," Samuel Johnson once remarked, in speaking of his school-boy days, "whipped me very hard. Without that, sir, I should have done nothing." Balzac, who wrote so many novels, yet did not let one appear until it had undergone repeated revision, confessed that not only in boyhood but throughout the years of his literary labours he was tormented by longings for an existence of pleasure-seeking leisure. Through the lips of his famous character, Raphael de Valentin, here is what he says of himself:

"Since the age of reason until the day when I had finished my task, I observed, read, wrote without ceasing, and my life was like a long imposition; an effeminate lover of oriental indolence, enamoured of my dreams, sensual, I have always worked, refusing to allow myself to taste the joys of Parisian life; gourmand, I have been temperate; enjoying movement and sea voyages, longing to visit other countries, still finding pleasure, like a child, in making ducks and drakes on the water, I remained constantly seated, pen in hand."

Taking into consideration facts like these, the evidence would certainly seem to be in favour of the view that, in yielding to a desire for idleness, men are, after all, only following the dictate of Nature. But, recalling the intense activity, the abounding energy of childhood, recalling also the demonstrable truth that in most cases even the laziest of school-boys has had a past characterised by the reverse of laziness, just as he may have, like

Darwin, Lyell, and the rest, a future of marvellous accomplishment, the mind must once more incline to the opposite belief.

It may be, and, as will be shown, it undoubtedly is, somewhat of an exaggeration to say that there never has been a congenitally lazy man. But to say this is far nearer the truth than to regard laziness as something rooted in the constitution of our being, and love of activity as merely an acquired characteristic. On the contrary, the sharp contrast between the activity and energy of the average child and the idling propensities of the average man, points unmistakably to the development of laziness as a parasitic growth interfering with the normal processes and tendencies of nature. Laziness, in other words, must be looked upon as essentially a pathological condition.

Instead, therefore, of condemning the lazy man, as the moralists would, it is the part of wisdom to view him as a victim of disease and as standing in need of careful treatment. Nature intended him to be vigorous, forceful, a being of achievement; circumstances have made him listless, inert, responsive but in feeble measure to the spur of honour, ambition, pride, love, or necessity. Sometimes, to be sure, he is contented with his laziness, and would almost resent an attempt to rescue him from it; more frequently he writhes in secret over a defect which he realises exposes him to the contempt and ridicule of his more virile fellow-men, and renders his life an empty, profitless existence. As one unhappy victim confessed in a moment of extraordinary self-revelation:

"I begin, but do not finish. When I conceive a work, a feverish impatience seizes me to reach the desired aim; I should like to attain it at once. But to accomplish something, patient and continuous efforts are required. I never accomplish anything.... One dull day, in one of the suburbs, I saw a large piece of waste land, more covered with fragments of earthenware than with grass. Three or four houses had been commenced, charming little dwellings of red brick and white stone; the walls had been there for two or three years, but the floors and ceilings were lacking, the roofs had never been tiled, and one could see across the ever wide-open windows. My mind is in a similar condition—a rough plain with several pretty houses, the roofs of which will never be finished." (*The Fortnightly Review*, vol. lxix, p. 763.)

What, then, is the cause of laziness? How should one proceed in the attempt to cure it? Still more important in this complex and severely competitive age, with its incessant demand for vigour and effectiveness of performance, what are the preventive measures that may be taken in the interest alike of the individual and society?

Only a few years ago it would have been impossible to answer these questions in any but the vaguest and most general way. It might have been said—indeed, it was said—that laziness is essentially an infirmity of the will. No statement could be more correct, but also none could be more futile in the absence of any clear appreciation of the factors determining the weakness or strength of one's will-power. For, as somebody has truly said, the will is not an isolated entity, absolutely independent of, and superior to, the organism through which it operates. Having a controlling force, it still is, to a large extent, itself controlled by material as well as by psychical circumstances, by bodily states and by the impressions the mind absorbs from the environment. Consequently the solution of the problem of laziness depends at bottom on the ascertainment of the factors hurtful to efficient willing.

This task quite recently has been essayed with remarkable success, and, especially by a little group of French investigators, with immediate reference to the problem presented by the lazy man. Laziness in all its phases has been studied with the resourcefulness and painstaking precision characteristic of the new school of medical psychologists, to whom we are already so heavily indebted for a better understanding of the mind of man both in its normal and its abnormal aspects. And with respect to laziness they have likewise made some interesting and important discoveries.

What, in particular, they have found is that it is usually associated with a peculiarly debilitated condition of the nervous system—an "asthenia" marked by a slow heart-beat, low arterial pressure, and poor circulation. The consequence of this is, to quote Théodule Ribot, one of the leaders in the scientific study of laziness, that "the brain shows not so much an indisposition as a real incapacity for concentrating attention, and soon, owing to the fact that its nourishment is at the vanishing-point, becomes exhausted." A whole series of idlers, tested scientifically, were shown to be suffering from this asthenic condition, which led them instinctively to husband their feeble resources by the simple expedient of exerting themselves no more than was absolutely necessary. Yet not a few of them were to all appearance healthy enough, and, until the medical examination had been made, it was difficult to credit their well-grounded complaint that they really felt "too tired to work," and at best could do so "only by fits and starts."

This is not to say that they were all of them "born tired." Congenitally weak many of them may have been; but the more the investigators familiarised themselves with the asthenia of the lazy, the more they found reason for the belief that, as a rule, it was an acquired and functional rather than an inborn and organic weakness, although often initiated by local troubles organic in nature. Thus, studying laziness in children attending school, it was discovered that quite frequently their inertia is connected with the presence of adenoid, or abnormal tissue, growths, in the cavity back of the nose. These growths, by making it extremely hard for the child to breathe properly, deplete his vitality so that he remains undersized and is quickly fatigued by intellectual or muscular effort. The natural consequence is that he becomes more or less of an idler, bringing upon himself the reproaches and punishments of parents and teachers. What he actually needs is not scoldings or whippings but a slight surgical operation.

Often a surprising development of both mental and physical power follows the removal of the adenoids. In one case, reported by Professor Swift, a girl of fourteen grew three inches taller within six months after an operation for adenoids, and at the same time showed an improvement in her school-work that contrasted strikingly with the apathy and dulness that had preceded it. Another, three years younger, grew six inches in about four months, and from being a sad idler was transformed into an unexpectedly attractive and bright pupil. A boy of twelve, backward both mentally and physically, likewise lost his dulness and laziness within an astonishingly short time after the impediment to his breathing had been removed.

Dental defects also contribute materially to the development of laziness and mental retardation. This has been repeatedly demonstrated in individual cases, and at least one psychologist—Professor J. E. Wallace Wallin, of St. Louis—has demonstrated it in the case of a group of children.

These children, twenty-seven in number, were pupils in a Cleveland public school; they were afflicted with tooth-decay to a varying extent, and they were mentally backward, being from one to four years retarded in their school-work. At Professor Wallin's direction their teeth and gums were treated, they were taught to use a tooth-brush properly, and to chew their food thoroughly. Before the dental treatment began they were twice given five psychological tests, to ascertain their memory-power, attention-power, etc.; the same tests were twice given to them while the treatment was under way; and, six months after its termination, or just before the close of the school-year 1910–1911, the tests were again given twice.

Comparing the results of the different testings, a progressive and remarkable improvement was found. In ability to memorise, the average improvement for the group was 19 per cent.; in attention power, 60 per cent.; in adding, 35 per cent.; in ability to associate words having an opposite meaning, 129 per cent.; and in general association ability, 42 per cent. More than this, and testifying incontrovertibly to the direct influence of the dental treatment in promoting vigour of thought, only one of the children failed of promotion, six completed thirty-eight weeks of school-work in twenty-four weeks, and one boy did two years' work in one year. Yet all of these children, remember, had formerly been quite unable to keep up with the work of their grades.

How explain this great improvement? Only on the theory that, by repairing their teeth and drilling them in the rudiments of mouth hygiene, a stop had been put to a disease-process which involved both nervous strain and—through the swallowing of the toxic products of tooth-decay—a poisoning of the supply of blood to the brain, with consequent lessening of the brain's ability to function properly.

Eye trouble, particularly in the way of hypermetropia, or far-sightedness, is another frequent cause of laziness in school-children, and the correction of the defective vision often is followed by a marked access of vigour and alertness. In such cases, however, the laziness is usually manifest only in the school-room, the child being active enough at play, when no strain is put on the eyes comparable with that occasioned by reading.

To cite a single instance, a little boy of ten was reported as being so inattentive at school and so uninterested in his work as to yawn and become sleepy when required to read. As no amount of scolding sufficed to turn him from his idle ways, and as he began to complain of headaches and nervousness, he was finally taken to an oculist. To the surprise of his parents, who had always believed his vision normal, he was found to be suffering from latent hypermetropia; and, on being provided with the proper eye-glasses, he soon demonstrated, by the rapidity with which he improved in his studies and the interest he now showed in them, that his laziness had been determined by the condition of his eyesight.

In fact, any bodily defect that is of such a character as to impose an excessive strain on the nervous system tends to produce an asthenic condition, with accompanying apathy and indolence. And, even when the local trouble is only temporary, its disappearance is not necessarily followed, as it was in the instances just narrated, by a return to energetic, effective activity. For, in the meantime, the idler may have acquired an unconscious—or, to be more precise, a subconscious—belief that sustained exertion is and always must be beyond his powers. Thus a vicious circle is established, the belief in his incapacity causing him to act in such a way as to intensify the asthenic state, and the resultant increased feeling of debility operating, in its turn, to confirm and strengthen his erroneous belief. In other words, he is now suffering chiefly from a "fixed idea," and his condition is that of any psycho-neurotic patient.

On this point all who have made a scientific study of laziness are in substantial agreement. We must, flatly affirms the pioneer investigator Doctor Maurice de Fleury, "take the indolent for what they nearly always are—neuropaths; and neurosis for what it always is—bad habits of cerebral activity." The longer a man has been an idler, the more deeply rooted, of course, will be his subconscious conviction that exertion is impossible to him; but, according to de Fleury and other investigators, once this conviction is broken down, he will find that he can work, and work to good purpose.

The effecting of a cure, needless to say, is not always easy. It requires co-operation on the part of the patient, and on the physician's part intelligent and sympathetic use of both physiological and psychological methods of treatment. Hygienic measures must be adopted to tone up the nervous system, to improve the circulation, the digestion, the nutrition—to develop, as far as possible, a general feeling of well-being. The idler must gradually be trained to occupy himself usefully—not, perhaps, for many hours at a time, but for regular stated periods, however short. And to this end, the effort has to be made, from the outset, to awaken in him an absorbing interest in the attainment of some one specific aim in life, thereby replacing his baneful fixed idea of incapacity for work with the opposed and beneficial obsession of something that he must and can accomplish.

Here we come to what is by far the most important factor in the cure of laziness—the dynamic, regenerative power of some special interest.[2] Even your idler, enfeebled by positive organic weakness, may rise superior to himself and achieve marvels, if only his enthusiasm be sufficiently aroused to a definite end. It was thus, for example, with Charles Darwin.

When he was a boy, as was said above, Darwin was colossally lazy. He neglected his books, and spent his days roaming through the fields, gun in hand. "You care for nothing but shooting, dogs, and rat-catching, and you will be a disgrace to yourself and all your family," was his father's bitter reproof. As he grew older, his propensity for idling seemed only to increase. In spite of this, hoping against hope that he would yet settle down to serious things, his father entered him at the University of Glasgow, with the idea of fitting him for the practice of medicine. "It is no use," the boy frankly avowed, after a few months at Glasgow; "I hate the work here, and I cannot possibly be a physician." So earnest were his protests that he was transferred to Cambridge University, on the understanding that he would study to be a clergyman.

At Cambridge, as good fortune would have it, he entered the natural history class of an eminent and enlightened scholar, Professor Henslow, who sent him into the woods and fields to make collections of plants and insects. Free again to roam under the clear blue skies, but this time with a lofty purpose set before his mind, a passion for achievement took possession of him. The boy whom other teachers had found dull and lazy proved himself, under Professor Henslow's inspiring guidance, a marvel of industry and mental vigour. There was no longer any thought of the "last resort" plan of putting him into the ministry. He would, he told his delighted father, become a naturalist, and he would work hard.

And he did work hard. Though his health was permanently impaired by the hardships of a voyage of exploration, so that "for nearly forty years he never knew one day of the health of ordinary men," and "every day succumbed to the exhaustion brought on by the slightest effort," he nevertheless found a way to work with an effectiveness few men of normal health have equalled.

The establishment of regular hours for work—thus gradually forming a work habit which itself constituted a sort of fixed idea contrary to the idea of indolence, and the reinforcement of this work habit by enthusiastic pre-occupation with an inspiring theme—such was the secret of Charles Darwin's mastery over ills more serious than those which have made countless men lifelong idlers. What he did is precisely what the medical psychologist of to-day prescribes as fundamental in the successful treatment of laziness. Listen to the wise Doctor de Fleury:

"Let it be known that it is often possible in the practice of life to replace an absurd idea by a good fixed one, and to form excellent habits in the place of deplorable manias. It is precisely in doing this that the psychological treatment of indolence consists; it is this patient work that the doctor of misguided minds ought to undertake.

"To induce [a lazy person] to become possessed of a good fixed idea, is not a superhuman work for those who know how to set about it. In fact, the means to be employed remind one of a woman who wishes to make herself loved.

"Let us consider for a moment the means dictated to her by her infallible instinct concerning love affairs. First of all, she dresses herself with care, so as to show off her charms to the full; then she finds opportunities for constantly being seen, increases the number of meetings; her presence must become habitual—in fact, necessary; he must suffer when she is no longer near. She kindles the flame of jealousy, to make it understood that she is an incomparable treasure, and that another will grasp her if he does not stretch forth his arm in time.

"Imitate her, you who wish to learn the marvellous art of reclaiming the indolent. Help your patient to choose a work really suited to his abilities; embellish the idea [of it] with all the hope that it is possible to raise—self-content, worldly importance, glory, and fortune to be conquered. Talk about it without ceasing; like a Wagnerian motive, repeat it again and again, and soon you will find that the brain seizes the idea, and can no longer exist without this good obsession. Finally, when the idea becomes cherished, when the brain loves it as one loves and desires a woman, make it to be understood that it belongs to all, that it is in the air, that another, braver and more manly, may step in and carry it off....

"Naturally, it is necessary to vary one's advice according to the character and profession of each patient. I have had the opportunity of treating—for nervous affections and at the same time for indolence—men occupying the most varied social positions: students, composers, military officers, men of letters, lawyers, financiers, politicians, poor workmen, and idle, rich people. For each one of them it was necessary to choose a ruling idea, suited to his occupation and in proportion to his strength."

Treatment by suggestion, then, plus careful preliminary physiological, and if necessary medical, treatment to ameliorate the asthenic condition common to idlers—that is the proper course to pursue in dealing with all cases of laziness. And it is also the course to pursue in the more important matter of prevention, a matter which, as the case of Charles Darwin strikingly suggests, rests chiefly with fathers and mothers.

Everybody knows that, as things now stand, young men and women choose vocations in a haphazard way, and too often choose vocations for which Nature has not intended them. What it is equally important to recognise is that even when they do happen to hit on a vocation fitted to them, it is only the exceptional man or woman who works anywhere near the limit of his or her capacity. The great majority fritter away much of their time, and may justly be accused of idleness.

The surprising thing about this is that, as has already been pointed out, it is seldom one sees anything like real laziness in early childhood. What causes the sharp contrast between the activity of childhood and the frequent apathy of later years? Unfavourable physical conditions cannot be held wholly responsible, especially when it is observed that there always are some people who, like Darwin, contrive to work effectively despite serious physical shortcomings. One must look a little deeper, and, looking deeper, one finds, as medical psychologists have lately found, that the trouble lies mostly with the parental attitude in childhood and youth.

Too many parents discourage the ceaseless questioning of their children, and thereby deaden that great stimulus to effort—curiosity. Too many fail to direct their children's thoughts into really worth while channels. Too many daily give them an example, not of industrious activity, but of half-hearted endeavour. All this goes to create in the child habits inimical to real work; and in proportion as he is afterward, by parent or teacher, forced to work, he finds work burdensome and exhausting. Under this condition, whether or no he is suffering from adenoids, eye trouble, or any other physical cause of nervous strain, he is likely to develop the asthenic state of the true idler, with the result of soon or late feeling that sustained effort is beyond him.

On parents, therefore, ultimately rests the blame for the prevalence of laziness; and for its prevention we must likewise look to parents. As a friend, a prominent American medical psychologist, once said to me emphatically:

"There would be far fewer lazy men in the world if parents only appreciated the possibility of so influencing their children in early youth as to confirm them in the tendencies to energetic action and fruitful thinking which they usually display in the first years of life. Instead of neglecting or repressing these tendencies, as so many parents unfortunately do, they should encourage their children in the active use of their minds, should train them in habits of systematic and effective thinking, and especially, by observing just what aptitudes they most clearly show, should take pains to cultivate in them an abiding interest in the subjects for which they seem to have greatest talent.

"If they would only do this, and would at the same time keep a close watch for any symptoms of nerve-strain due to organic or functional disturbances, correcting these at the earliest possible moment, we should hear much less than we do now of the indolence of the average child of school age; and we certainly should be taking a great forward step in the lessening of laziness among grown men and women. For, obviously, a child habituated from infancy to the fullest and freest use of his natural powers, will be likely to continue thinking and acting energetically in later life. In this, as in everything else, the law is the same—as the twig is bent, the tree's inclined."

VI

A CHAPTER ON LAUGHTER

Picture to yourself a familiar scene—the interior of a theatre crowded with people. On the stage the persons of the play move to and fro, speaking their lines. Presently a slight change is made in the current of the dialogue, and, presto! the spectators who have been so quietly listening and watching become weirdly agitated. Their features are distorted in strange grimaces, they throw back their heads, and give utterance to abrupt, explosive, unmelodious noises. Even their bodies take part in the amazing commotion.

Something "funny" has just been said by one of the actors, and those who have heard it are responding by an outburst of "laughter."

Recall likewise the equally familiar picture of a huge circus tent with its bewildering array of equipment for the performance of feats of strength and daring, surrounded by tier upon tier of seats filled with expectant holiday-makers. The entertainment is about to begin; from an entrance come the blaring strains of a brass band, and a long, gaily bedecked procession circles slowly before the gaping throng. At the end of the procession are half a dozen men of uncouth gait and bizarre appearance, their faces whitened and spotted, queer conical caps on their heads, and wearing enormous, shapeless garments as white and spotted as their faces.

These men say nothing—they simply go through all sorts of foolish antics. But at the mere sight of them the same uproar of discordant sounds fills the air, the spectators, like those of the theatre and with even greater vehemence, uniting in a very bedlam of guffaws.

Pass, finally, to the open street, alive with men and women hurrying to their work. Some one has carelessly dropped on the sidewalk the slippery skin of a fruit. The first man to step on it feels his legs give way beneath him, strives frantically to keep his balance, waves his arms about, and ends by plumping to the ground with a heavy thud. At once he is beset by the "smiles" and "chuckles" of those who have witnessed his fall; and, hurt and annoyed, he scrambles to his feet, gives himself a hasty brush, and disappears as rapidly as possible.

Now, just what is this singular phenomenon of laughter, so readily induced and from such a variety of causes? What is there in the words of an actor, the antics of a clown, or the misfortune of another person, to provoke, under the circumstances mentioned, the peculiar reaction of bodily and facial contortion and inarticulate vocal utterance that, regarded dispassionately, seems almost repulsive? What useful purpose can be served by such behaviour, such an obvious departure from the well-ordered ways of the reasoning life? In a word, why do we laugh?

It is a question far more easily asked than answered, as every one has discovered who has really pondered it. The answer that immediately comes to mind—"We laugh because we are amused"—not only is hopelessly inadequate, but to a large extent is incorrect. It can readily be shown that people sometimes laugh in situations where their mental state is anything but that of amusement. In one well-authenticated instance a frontiersman, on returning to his home and finding it in ruins, with his wife and children mutilated corpses, began to laugh and continued laughing until he died from the rupture of a blood-vessel. In another case, cited among the responses to a questionnaire on laughter issued by that well-known American psychologist, President G. Stanley Hall of Clark University, a number of young people from nineteen to twenty-four years of age were sitting together when the death of a friend was announced. "They looked at each other for a second, and then all began to laugh, and it was some time before they could become serious."

A young woman, replying to the same questionnaire, confessed that she often laughed when hearing people speak of the death of their friends, "not because it is funny or pleases her, but because she cannot help it." Another young woman reported that on hearing of the death of a former school-mate she felt deeply grieved, yet "laughed as heartily as she had ever done in her life," and, in spite of every effort to control herself, "had to break out into a laugh repeatedly." A third "must always laugh when she hears of a death, and has had to leave the church at a funeral because she must giggle."

Even the shock of a severe physical pain is known to provoke occasionally, not tears but laughter. "A young man," says C. G. Lange, "whom I was treating with a powerful caustic for an ulceration of the tongue, invariably, at the moment when the pain was at its highest, was attacked by a violent outburst of laughter."

One has only to think also of the laughter caused by tickling to realise that it is not always true to say that we laugh because we are amused. And when it is true, this answer, instead of solving the problem of laughter, merely raises it in another form, since it then becomes necessary to explain why we are amused by the sayings and happenings at which we laugh. Most students of laughter have indeed felt that the important thing to do is to determine the nature of the laughable, a task itself of considerable difficulty and leading to the most diverse conclusions in the numerous explanatory formulas which have been advanced from time to time, but which, when closely scrutinised, are chiefly noteworthy for their incompleteness.

To mention only a few of the theories of the comic finding place in psychological works, it is affirmed by some authorities that the essence of the laughable is that it induces a sudden sense of superiority in the person moved to laughter. This is the "sudden glory" theory of Thomas Hobbes, and in support of it is cited more especially the familiar fact that nobody likes to be laughed at. It also finds support in the undoubted feeling of contempt which so often accompanies the laughter provoked by the buffooneries of a mountebank, the dialogue and action of a farce comedy, and the so-called "comic pictures" now to be found in such lamentable profusion in many of our newspapers. In some slight degree, too, there may be a "sudden glory" in the laughter at the awkwardness and groundless fears of a child, or at his naïve remarks, and in the laughter occasioned by mischances to other people. But certainly there is much that is laughable—notably the kindly banter between friends—that cannot reasonably be said to engender any feeling of superiority. And, more than this, we are all of us, every day of our lives, witnessing things that do suddenly arouse in us a lively feeling of superiority, but without moving us to laughter—moving us, rather, to pity and perhaps tears.

Even as amended by the psychologist Bain, the "sudden glory" theory remains inadequate. Bain defines "the occasion of the ludicrous" as "the degradation of some person or interest possessing dignity in circumstances that excite no other strong emotion." This is a decided improvement, because it clearly recognises that the laughable must be devoid of elements awakening counteracting emotions. But it is open to the criticism that laughter is frequently excited by objects and occurrences in which, unless the imagination be severely wrenched, it is impossible to assume that ideas of degradation are dominant or even operant.

When, for example, we laugh at the spectacle of a child half hidden in his grandfather's hat, what do we think of as degraded? Is it the child, the hat, or the absent grandfather? In such an instance can the idea of degradation properly be said to enter at all? So, likewise, it is difficult to conceive the presence of any idea either of degradation or superiority in the ringing laughter of a child at his puppy's gambols or at the frisking of his kitten. And how explain on such a principle the laughter at non-malicious witticism?

Appreciating the inapplicability of the Hobbesian doctrine in any form as explanatory of all sources of laughter, other investigators have emphasised the principle of contrast and incongruity, but to scarcely more satisfactory effect. "Laughter," says Herbert Spencer, "naturally results only when consciousness is unawares transferred from great things to small—when there is what we call a descending incongruity." The manifest insufficiency of this theory is avoided in the more extensive one, to which Darwin inclines, defining the laughable as that which is queer, unusual, disagreeing with or contrary to our mental habits or the normal order of affairs. Assuredly there is almost always an element of queerness in the things at which we laugh. Yet it is also certain that the queer does not always make us laugh. As Camille Mélinaud has pointed out:

"There are things contrary to the normal order that have nothing ludicrous about them; and if the view were true that queerness is the laughable element, those things that are strangest and most unusual should be the ones most certain by their very nature to excite laughter. But we do not laugh at the dancing horses, the jumping pigs, the musicians playing on bottles, of the circus, all of which are most contradictory of what we are accustomed to. If we laugh at the circus, it is at the accessory jokes and incidents in the detail. A conjurer's tricks, seemingly contradictory as they are of all our experiences and notions, do not make us laugh. We laugh at his jokes and his funny ways of proceeding, but we wonder at his tricks." (*Popular Science Monthly*, vol. liii, p. 398.)

Mélinaud's own view, oddly enough, is about as unconvincing as any that has ever been formulated, for, while laying stress on the principle of incongruity, he insists that laughter comes only when the laugher, "by a rapid process of thought," submits the object of his mirth to a reflective analysis and arrives at the laugh-provoking conclusion that what seems absurd is really quite natural from the point of view of the person or thing laughed at. Then, and not until then, do we feel amused. On such a theory one might well wonder that children ever find it possible to laugh, and that laughter is so prevalent among adults who are not accustomed to any very high degree of logical thinking.

Altogether different from any of the foregoing is the more recent theory of the French philosopher, Henri Bergson, as presented in a special treatise on laughter, of which an excellent translation by C. Brereton and F. Rothwell has lately been published in this country. Bergson recognises, as not every investigator has done, the essentially spontaneous character of laughter, and he insists with Darwin on postulating queerness as an indispensable element in the laughable. But, as he sees it, the queerness must be of a specific sort in order to excite laughter—must consist, in fine, in an automatic inelasticity, whether of form, action, or thought, which is in sharp contrast to the wonted mobility of life. It is our immediate recognition of this automatism and rigidity that moves us to laughter.

When, Bergson affirms, we laugh at a man who stumbles and falls in the street, our laughter is caused, not by his sudden change of attitude, but by the involuntary element in this change. "Perhaps there was a stone on the road. He should have altered his pace or avoided the obstacle. Instead of that, through lack of elasticity, through absent-mindedness and a kind of physical obstinacy—as a result, in fact, of rigidity or of momentum—the muscles continued to perform the same movement when the circumstances of the case called for something else. That is the reason of the man's fall, and also of the people's laughter." So with our laughter at the appearance and horseplay of a clown. We laugh at his painted face because we immediately recognise in it "something mechanical encrusted upon the living," and we laugh at his antics because of their automatic, machine-like character.

In fact, "We laugh every time a person gives us the impression of being a thing. We laugh at Sancho Panza tumbled into a bed-quilt and tossed into the air like a foot-ball. We laugh at Baron Munchausen turned into a cannon-ball and travelling through space." In laughter caused by puns, jests, and witticisms, the same principles of automatism and inelasticity obtain, though of course in much subtler form. Analyse closely all varieties of the comic and you always get back to the basic idea of "something mechanical in something living." Or, Bergson concludes, "The comic is that side of a person which reveals his likeness to a thing, that aspect of human events which, through its peculiar inelasticity, conveys the impression of pure mechanism, of automatism, of movement without life."

Really to appreciate both the plausibility and the shortcomings of this novel theory of the laughable one must read Professor Bergson's book. It is there elaborated so ingeniously that one finds it difficult to give instances of the comic to which it cannot in some way be applied. Even the laughter of children at the bobbing up of their jack-in-the-box, the fall of their house of cards, or the tail-chasing gyrations of their kitten, may conceivably be explained on the assumption that what the children laugh at is the automatic character of the bobbing, the falling, and the whirling. On the other hand, these very examples irresistibly suggest that the Bergsonian explanation is, after all, rather strained and far-fetched, and that, in common with its less thorough-going predecessors, it overlooks the elusive something fundamental to the laughable. This impression is deepened when we recall the extent to which automatism, rigidity, inelasticity, prevail in the affairs of men without exciting so much as a smile.

"The attitudes, gestures, and movements of the human body," says Professor Bergson, in stating one of his many subsidiary laws of the comic, "are laughable in exact proportion as that body reminds us of a mere machine." Why, then, do we not laugh when we observe the machine-like precision with which a company of soldiers march on parade or execute the evolutions of drill? Surely one could not find a better example of "something mechanical in something living." And, again, "any arrangement of acts and events is comic which gives us, in a single combination, the illusion of life and the distinct impression of a mechanical arrangement." The bobbing of the jack-in-the-box meets this formula, and we do laugh at the jack-in-the-box. But it is met equally well by the strangely lifelike movements of such devices as the automatic chess-player and the typesetting machine, yet these do not ordinarily elicit any appreciable manifestation of mirth.

It is, however, when we turn to Bergson's deductions from his theory of the comic that we are most strongly impelled to question its soundness. Emphasizing as he does the element of automatism in the laughable, he logically enough infers that the function of laughter is to serve as a social corrective. "The rigid, the ready-made, the mechanical, in contrast with the supple, the ever-changing, and the living, absent-mindedness in contrast with attention, in a word, automatism in contrast with free activity, such are the defects that laughter singles out and would fain correct." We laugh, that is to say, only at imperfections in our fellow-men, or at things which remind us of imperfections, and the reason we laugh is that, consciously or unconsciously, we wish to call attention to them by way of, in Bergson's own words, "a kind of social ragging."

Stated thus baldly, the underlying defect of such an explanation of laughter becomes plainly apparent.[3] What has happened is that its author has read into the phenomenon of laughter a meaning applicable only under special circumstances. If it were true that we laugh only at what is imperfect and therefore ugly, however attenuated in ugliness, it would be impossible to understand the well-nigh universal eagerness for laughter; an eagerness which has led mankind to reward lavishly, even extravagantly, those who make it their business to provide occasions for laughter—the writers of farces and comedies, the fun-making actors and clowns, the producers of "comic pictures." The egregious falsity of this "deformity" theory, as it may fairly be called, becomes still more manifest when we endeavour to apply it to account for the laughter of childhood, the period of life when laughter is most free and exuberant, but precisely when it is incredible to assume that it is motivated by any corrective impulse, conscious or otherwise.

To tell the truth, the attempt to reach a wholly satisfactory solution of the problem of laughter by striving to define the characteristics of the laughable seems foredoomed to failure. For, after all, the laughable must always remain a more or less uncertain quantity, if only for the reason that, as shown by facts of everyday observation, what makes one person laugh may not be in the least laugh-provoking to another. Yet everybody, or almost everybody, does laugh to some extent, and therefore the proper point of approach would rather seem to be through a study of the act of laughter itself and of its consequences with regard, not to the person or thing or phrase laughed at, but to the person doing the laughing.

Attacking the problem from this altogether different angle, one is soon in a position to discern several facts of real helpfulness in an explanatory way. By no means the least important is the extreme exuberance of laughter in childhood, to which reference has just been made. Once the child has begun to laugh—usually during the fourth or fifth month after birth, although occasional outbursts of a shadowy sort of laughter have been observed before the fourth month—it laughs with a truly amazing spontaneity and frequency. There seems to be nothing which may not become an object of laughter to a child, and, more than this, in direct contradiction to all theories postulating a reflective element at the bottom of every laugh, as often as not the laughter of childhood is conspicuously devoid of such an element.

For example, to cite a few observations from the record of a lady, Miss Milicent Shinn, whose painstaking study of the infancy of her niece Ruth is among the most stimulating of contributions to the modern science of child psychology, it appears that toward the end of the fifth month this little girl "habitually laughed with glee when any one smiled or spoke to her." And when, two months later, she was taken into the open and allowed to roll about on a quilt, "the wooing of the passing freshness, the play of sun and shadow, the large stir of life in moving and sounding things, all this possessed her and made her 'laugh and ejaculate with pleasure.'" Also, like almost every child of her age, little Ruth would be moved to hilarious mirth by being given a ride on somebody's foot, or tossed and jumped about in one's arms. Laughter, again, followed the successful accomplishment of any intellectual or muscular feat, such as pointing out pictures she had been asked to identify, climbing stairs, or deliberately letting herself fall "so as to come down sitting with a thud."

The same tendency to excessive, even seemingly causeless laughter in the opening years of life has been noted by other close students of the emotions and their expression. Some have attempted, with the usual futile results, to explain it by an analysis of the things at which the child laughs. Others, more cautiously and more accurately, content themselves with describing it as a means whereby Nature provides a salutary outlet for surplus nervous energy.

It is undoubtedly this. Ask any child who has learned to talk—or, better, ask a grown person who has retained to a marked degree the faculty for hearty laughter—and the chances are you will be told that, while in any given instance the laugher may be far from clear as to why he has laughed, he does know that the involuntary movements of the laughter to which he yielded were preceded by peculiarly compelling sensations, variously expressed in such phrases as, "I had to laugh or burst," "I had to do something to relieve the strain," "I felt bubbling over," "I felt a quiver, a thrill, a creepy feeling passing from my stomach to my mouth."

That is to say, the evidence from the abounding laughter of childhood—pre-eminently a period of rapid physical growth and of the accumulation of a large store of nervous energy—as also the evidence from the laughter of unusually mirthful adults, who are, as a rule, persons of large build and of corresponding nervous force, suggests irresistibly the conception of laughter as an instinct implanted in us for the performance of an important physiological function. This view finds additional support in the familiar "giggling silliness" of the adolescent period, that strange period of unusual growth and stress, and the one in which are most likely to occur those singular attacks of untimely hilarity at funerals and on other solemn occasions, as mentioned among the responses to President Hall's questionnaire. No more than the little child or your friend the jolly man does the adolescent always know at what he is laughing. He simply knows that he is impelled to laugh by forces latent in his being and over which he has no control.

Nor is it only as a relief from neural tension that laughter benefits the one who laughs. In the studies of laughter in childhood made by such investigators as Preyer, Sully, and Miss Shinn, one finds frequent allusion to occasions when laughter is obviously a reaction from a state of mental strain, and has a specifically useful effect in easing the mind. There is reason to believe that this is actually one of its constant ends—that it is a device for lightening the burden of mentation by temporary interruption of the thought process.

As all educators are well aware, the first years of life and the adolescent period are not only the years of greatest physical growth, but the years when the severest demands are made on the mind, both by the task of acquiring knowledge and by the perturbations of adolescence. They are the years when the mind, in its immaturity, is most in need of some protective mechanism to enable it automatically and at frequent intervals to take a holiday as it were. Such a mechanism is admirably provided in laughter, which, as every laugher will at once appreciate, when not unduly prolonged leaves behind it a pleasurable feeling of exhilaration and greater mental as well as physical well-being.

We laugh, then, in infancy and adolescence, not primarily because we are "light-hearted" or "amused," but to satisfy a natural instinct of both physiological and psychological utility. We laugh less in maturity, partly because we have not, as a rule, the same necessity of getting rid of surplus nervous energy, partly because our minds have passed the tender formative age, and partly because widening experience has developed sentiments and ideas tending to inhibit laughter. Nevertheless we do still need to a certain extent the relief which laughter brings; we feel in some degree the old hunger for it, and consequently, often at very slight provocation, we yield, and even cultivate opportunities for yielding, to the impulse which was so conspicuously operant in the years of our youth. As with every instinct, moreover, the laughing process may, and occasionally does, become perverted, as in the laughter of cynicism and contempt, and in the abnormal laughter of the overwrought—itself, however, the modern medical psychologist assures us, a medium of relief from an unbearable strain.

As to the things at which we commonly laugh—the "laughable" whose nature has so perplexed philosophers—all that may safely be said is that their laugh-provoking power depends not so much on an inherent "comicality" as on the circumstances under which they occur to us, and our point of view toward them as determined by previous training and experience. Certainly, for instance, we cannot laugh at a subtle bit of wit until we have had education in the appreciation of the skilful use of language. The instincts of imitation and of sympathy, further, have a share in determining on many an occasion the functioning of the laughing instinct. Time and again we laugh merely because we see other people laughing. Personally I am inclined to think also that much at which we laugh as adults is laughable to us only by reason of subconscious association with similar occurrences which chanced to move us to laughter in our childhood. But on this point nothing positive should be asserted pending psychological investigation which has yet to be made.

Conceding, however, that the laughable is and must always remain elusive, baffling, uncertain, there need be no uncertainty as to our view of laughter itself. To laugh—to laugh spontaneously and heartily—is under nearly every circumstance a good thing both for the body and for the mind. Like sleep, it refreshes; like food, it strengthens. Humanity in truth would be the poorer—and the shorter-lived—were it ever to lose this splendid heritage of the power to laugh.

This is why I have said so much about laughter in the present book. To parents in especial knowledge of its true significance is important. They will not then fall into the mistake, too often made at present, of curbing their children's instinctive tendency to laugh. Rather, they should deliberately seek to cultivate in them a keen sense of humour, and encourage them in merriment—not because it is a thing pleasing in itself, but because of its positive developmental value. Directly or indirectly to repress this basic instinct is always dangerous, leading to warpings of character, and at times undoubtedly contributing to the causation of that strangest and most misunderstood of human maladies, hysteria, to which we must now give some consideration.

VII

HYSTERIA IN CHILDHOOD

A little girl, a pupil in a German school, made her appearance in class one morning with a bandage about her head. In answer to her teacher's questions, she said she had been operated upon for ear trouble at a local hospital the day before. She described every detail of the operation, which, it seemed, had been exceedingly painful.

For some time she wore the bandage to school every day, and frequently complained that her ear was still troubling her. Her teacher was properly sympathetic, and, chancing to meet one of the girl's relatives, expressed her anxiety for the child, and the hope that she would soon be completely cured.

"Cured?" repeated the relative. "Cured of what?"

"Why, her ear trouble—the disease that has made it necessary for her to keep her head bandaged."

"But," said the other, obviously puzzled, "I do not understand you. I did not know she had any ear trouble, and I have never seen her with a bandage."

It was the teacher's turn to be astonished. She could not believe that the girl had been deceiving her; but, to get at the truth, she decided to take her immediately to the hospital where the operation was supposed to have been performed. There the child made her way about as if perfectly familiar with the place, and greeted in a friendly manner the surgeon in charge. He, however, did not seem to recognise her, and when told the circumstances by the teacher, said:

"I can assure you I have never operated upon this girl."

He then made a thorough examination of her ear, and found it to be quite sound. After which, careful investigation developed the fact that her sole knowledge of the hospital was derived from detailed information given her by a friend, a lady who, curiously enough, had been operated upon a little while previously for precisely the trouble that the girl had attributed to herself.

In other words, no doubt remained that she had for weeks been acting a lie, from what motive neither her teacher nor her parents could fathom.

Again, a clergyman writing to the Society for Psychical Research from a little English village named Ham, urgently requested the despatch of a skilled investigator to look into certain strange occurrences in the house of a Mr. Turner. This house, the clergyman asserted, was haunted by a "veritable ghost," which amused itself by playing all sorts of mischievous and annoying pranks.

Remaining invisible, it hurled boots, shoes, and other small objects through the air, upset chairs and tables, and on at least one occasion it had pitched the family cat into the fire. All this was done, according to both the clergyman and several other intelligent eye-witnesses, under circumstances that rendered it impossible that the "manifestations" could be the work of any human agency.

"No one can explain it," the clergyman declared. "It is quite a mystery, and is causing great excitement through the countryside."

The task of laying this "poltergeist," or troublesome ghost, was assigned to Mr. Ernest Westlake, an able psychical researcher. Proceeding to Ham, he found that the Turner family consisted of Mr. Turner, his wife, one son, and a deformed little daughter, Polly, not quite twelve years old. So impressed was he with what he heard that his first report indicated a belief that the phenomena witnessed might be genuine evidences of some mysterious and unknown force. But, after a few hours of watchful scrutiny, he sent word that "the Ham ghost is a humbug *now*, whatever it may have been." In detail Mr. Westlake afterward added:

"After posting my first letter, I went to the Turners' and sat on a bench in front of the fire. No one else was present besides the child. She sat on a low stool in the chimney on the right of the fire. On the other side of the hearth there was a brick oven in which, much to Polly's interest, I placed a dish of flour, arguing that a power capable of discharging the contents of the oven (one of the first disturbances) might be able to impress the flour. After a time I went to the oven to see how the flour was getting on, stooping slightly to look in; but I kept my eye on the child's hands, looking at them under my right arm. I saw her hand stealing down toward a stick that was projecting from the fire; I moved slightly, and the hand was withdrawn.

Next time I was careful to make no movement, and saw her hand jerk the brand out on to the floor. She cried out. I expressed interest and astonishment; and her mother came in and cleared up the debris.

"This was repeated several times, and one or two large sticks ready for burning, which stood near the child, was thrown down. Then a kettle that was hanging on a hook and chain was jerked off the hook on to the coals. This was repeated. As the kettle refused to stay on its hook, the mother placed it on the hearth; but it was soon overturned on to the floor. After this, I was sitting on the bench that stood facing the fire in front of the table. I had placed my hat on the table behind me. The little girl was standing near me on my right hand. Presently the hat was thrown down on to the ground. I did not on the first occasion see the girl's movements; but later, by seeming to look in another direction, I saw her hand sweep the hat off on to the floor. This I saw at least twice. A Windsor chair near the girl was then upset more than once, falling away from her. On one occasion I saw her push the chair over with both hands. As she was looking away from me, I got a nearly complete view. After one of these performances, the mother came in and asked the child if she had done it; but the latter denied it." (*Proceedings of the Society for Psychical Research*, vol. xii.)

Unquestionably, Mr. Westlake concluded, Polly was the "ghost." Yet he found it difficult to conjecture why she should have assumed so singular a rôle. Neither she nor her parents—whom he exonerated from all complicity—had profited a penny's worth from her exploits. Indeed, her parents had been put out of pocket by the damage to the household furniture and utensils.

Consider, also, the case of a little Chicago boy who had fallen out of a play-wagon and hurt one of his arms. The injury was in reality very slight; but his mother, becoming greatly alarmed, declared her belief that the doctor would say the arm was broken. What the doctor—D'Orsay Hecht, of Northwestern University Medical School—did say was that a few applications of witch-hazel would speedily remedy matters.

The mother, nevertheless, insisted on bandaging the arm, talked of having an X-ray examination, and broadly hinted that a wrong diagnosis had been made. Within a few days, as Doctor Hecht had expected, all signs of injury disappeared. But now the boy complained that the hand of the injured arm felt stiff; and, in a day or so, his mother reported that both hand and arm were paralysed.

This was the situation when, passing along the street one day, Doctor Hecht was astonished and amused to see his "paralysed" patient romping with a number of children, quite as if nothing were the matter with him. He used his injured arm freely, pushed and pulled his playmates, and was pushed and pulled around by them.

"Ah," thought the physician, with a feeling of relief, "evidently this youngster is going to give no more trouble."

He was mistaken. Within a week the mother sent for him, reporting that her boy was suffering agonies, that he could not eat, and that his arm had become contracted at the elbow. In fact, on visiting the boy he found that at every attempt to flex the arm the little fellow screamed with pain.

But on his next visit, when the child chanced to be asleep, Doctor Hecht noticed that there was then no contracture of the arm, and that he could move it without disturbing the boy in the slightest. So soon, however, as he awoke, the contracture returned, and he wailed and shrieked when his arm was touched. To the astonished mother, the doctor said:

"I see what the trouble is. Your son needs a certain kind of treatment that I can administer only at my office. Bring him there as soon as possible."

The treatment in question consisted in the application of a succession of slight electrical shocks, just painful enough to be felt. These, the doctor assured the boy, would cure him completely.

"If they do not," said he, "your mother must bring you back, and I will give you a stronger treatment next time. I don't think, though, that that will be necessary, do you?"

And, in point of fact, no second treatment was needed. From that moment the boy ceased complaining of his arm, the contracture and paralysis entirely disappeared, and he was like any normal, healthy child.

I have cited these three cases, not because of their singularity, but because they afford concrete illustration of some little known facts with which every parent ought to be acquainted. In each case, it will be observed, an element of deception was present; and, moreover, in each case the deception was seemingly motiveless. The child who pretended that she had been operated upon had apparently nothing to gain from the deceit practised by her; neither had the little girl who played the part of a "poltergeist," nor the boy with the sham contracture and paralysis. Besides which, in two of the three cases the children subjected themselves to considerable inconvenience and even pain; and, in all three cases, they ran the risk of severe punishment. None the less, they systematically and persistently kept up their deceptions until discovery ensued.

Now, why did they do it?

They did it, as recent medical and psychological investigation into the inner life of childhood has conclusively demonstrated, because they were so constituted that they could not help doing it. And for the same reason, hundreds—nay, thousands—of children, before and since, have been doing much the same thing. It is not that they are merely "naughty." The ordinary naughty child will, to be sure, lie and cheat and otherwise deceive; but only from readily ascertainable motives, and never in the way of an elaborately sustained deception. When a child's "naughtiness" takes this latter form, medical authorities are to-day agreed, it is in reality indicative of the presence of a really serious disease—hysteria.

Than this disease—of which most people, unfortunately, have next to no exact knowledge, mistakenly confusing it with, and confining it to, uncontrollable attacks of weeping or laughing—there is no malady more insidious, peculiar, or dangerous in the variety of its possible consequences. Its peculiarity lies in the fact—discovered only within recent years—that it is always rooted in an extreme "suggestibility" on the part of its victims; and that the symptoms it develops are invariably conditioned by the character of the suggestions received from the environment. Hysteria is, to put the case briefly, pre-eminently a mental trouble; and this although, not infrequently, its only outward manifestations are wholly physical.

A child with a hysterical tendency—that is to say, an unusually sensitive, impressionable child, of undisciplined will, and quickly overwhelmed by whatever it sees, hears, or feels—is always liable, when brought into contact with a person suffering from any serious ailment of picturesque symptomatology, to manifest in some degree the symptoms of that particular ailment. Or, more commonly, such a child may manifest grave physical disabilities simply as a result of hearing or reading about them.

It does not do this voluntarily; there is no conscious intention to deceive; for the matter of that, the child itself is as much deceived as are its parents and friends. The trouble is that in its state of abnormal suggestibility, it is irresistibly impelled by the strange power of self-suggestion to imitate the symptoms of disease.

Or, instead of simulating disease symptoms, a hysterical child may enter on a course of seemingly deliberate chicanery like that practised by little "poltergeist" Polly Turner, whose case is typical of a species of behaviour indulged in by hysterical children in all countries and all ages. Here, likewise, abnormal suggestibility is in evidence, the resultant hysterical manifestations differing only because the suggestions received and acted on are different.

In cases like Polly Turner's, it has been found, the hysterical child usually lives with people more or less superstitious and credulous. They are people inclined to attribute to some spiritistic agency any occurrence they cannot easily explain. In this environment the child gradually becomes obsessed—though quite unconsciously—with a desire to provide "marvels" for their edification and mystification, and, yielding to the desire, is soon in full career as a "poltergeist," the hysterical obsession becoming intensified in proportion as the gullibility of those deceived increases, and also in proportion to the amount of attention paid to the little deceiver.

For—and this is a point to be borne well in mind—it is not alone abnormal suggestibility that characterises the hysterical child. There is also present an abnormal craving to attract attention, to be a centre of interest. Of this craving, as of the deceits carried out to attain its realisation, the child itself is unconscious. But it may be stated with assurance that it invariably exists as a concomitant of hysteria. Ordinarily it is the family and intimate friends whose interest and sympathy the child wishes to arouse, though this is not always the case. There may be special reasons for desiring to impress mere acquaintances, or even absolute strangers. Then we have the odd spectacle of children, like the pupil in the German school, whose hysterical obsessions appear chiefly or only in the presence of outsiders, while the parents remain in partial or total ignorance of them.

And, speaking of this type of hysteria, I may say that I am acquainted with a young New York woman who, since the age of fifteen, has led many an unsuspecting physician a merry dance by reason of her extraordinary hysterical simulations. In early girlhood she began to complain of various ailments, which on examination proved to be of no moment. Not unnaturally her family lost patience with her "whims," as they called them, and regarded her as a wholly imaginary invalid. Like most people similarly situated, they utterly failed to appreciate that, as has been well said by Doctor Pierre Janet, one of the world's foremost authorities on hysteria, "When a person is so ill that he says he is ill when he is not ill at all, then he must be very ill indeed." They scolded the girl, they argued with her; but they made no attempt to give her the treatment she really needed.

What was the consequence? One day she mysteriously disappeared from home, and some time passed before she was located in a hospital, where preparations were making to perform an operation upon her for appendicitis. A little later she wandered off again, and turned up at another hospital with symptoms so closely resembling a tumorous growth that a diagnosis to that effect was made, and an immediate operation advised. Still later an eminent specialist was misled into crediting her with a serious spinal disease.

After this it was decided that she was insane, and the family had her committed to an asylum. Before her release she developed symptoms of ear trouble so pronounced that the dangerous mastoid operation would have been performed had not the superintendent of the asylum been informed of her previous adventures as a hospital visitant.

Manifestly, a disease that both impels and enables its victims to mimic the symptoms of grave organic affections, with such verisimilitude as to deceive even physicians, is an extremely serious affair. And one has only to inquire of doctors with an extensive hospital experience to learn that hysteria, in one form or another, is a widespread trouble among both children and adults. But it is no longer the bugbear of the medical profession that it used to be. Following the discovery of its essentially mental character, methods have been devised and perfected for handling it. Some of these seem absurdly simple, but even the simplest have been proved efficacious, especially in the case of children. Differing in detail, they have one feature in common. They directly attack the hysterical symptoms by the employment of the same agency that was provocative of them—namely, suggestion.

In the case of the boy with the pseudo paralysis, reported above, it was not any therapeutic virtue inherent in the electrical treatment that brought about his rapid restoration to health. It was simply the suggestive efficacy of the way in which the treatment was administered to him. The truth of this, however, may be made clearer by the citation of one or two other cases, that are also of interest as illustrating the ingenious devices by which hysterical attacks in the period of childhood are nowadays overcome.

There was brought to a New England neurologist a little girl of ten, suffering from a curious physical abnormality. As long as she was seated, there seemed to be little the matter with her; but the moment she attempted to stand her feet bent under her so that they would not support her weight. When left alone she swayed backward and forward, and then fell on her hands and knees. In addition to this, there was a complete paralysis of the left arm, the child thus being deprived of the use of three of her four limbs.

Questioned by the physician, her mother explained that these muscular troubles had first set in six months before, following an attack of measles, and that her condition had grown progressively worse. This pointed to an organic and incurable malady; and, indeed, the mother was firmly convinced that nothing could be done. But, on making some delicate diagnostic tests, no signs of true organic trouble were to be found; whereas there were some indications that the disability might be wholly functional, the result of hysteria. In verification of his suspicion the physician made a few experiments which proved that the child was extremely suggestible. Turning to her mother, he said:

"You are quite wrong in supposing that your daughter cannot be cured. She is ill, it is true; but her illness is of such a nature that it will quickly respond to the right kind of treatment."

"But," protested the mother, incredulous, "she cannot use her legs, she cannot move her arm."

"No matter. I have something here that will enable her to use her legs and move her arm."

He took up a large magnet and showed it to the little girl. She watched him with the keenest interest, while he used it to lift several pieces of iron.

"Now look," said he.

Holding it over his left hand, he slowly raised that hand until it touched the magnet, pretending that it had been drawn up exactly as the pieces of iron had been.

"You see the power of this instrument," he said, to the wondering child. "It can move your arm, and give strength to your legs and feet, in the very same way."

For three weeks the magnet was applied to the different muscles, with the suggestion that the limbs would thereby regain their power. Nine treatments in all were given. After the ninth treatment the girl walked into the doctor's office unaided.

"Yesterday," her mother explained, "she told me that she thought her arm felt better, and she found that she could raise it. Then she said she believed she could walk; and, getting out of bed, she crossed the room without the least assistance, and without her feet clubbing under her. Can it be, Doctor, that she is cured?"

In fact, she was cured; although, of course, the magnet itself had had no power to cure her, but was used merely as an agent for an efficient "counter-suggestion" to dislodge and uproot the symptom-producing suggestions in the girl's own mind.

Excellent results have also been obtained in many cases of hysterical paralysis among children by the use of what is known as the "method of surprise," the invention of a German specialist named Bruns. As employed by Doctor Bruns and his followers, this method has undoubtedly a certain aspect of brutality; but this is more than compensated by its effectiveness. Having determined, by a searching medical examination, that the paralysis in any given case is functional and not organic, what Bruns does is to place the paralysed child in a bath-tub, turn on the cold water faucet, and watch the youngster climb out and scamper off.

"You see," he then says to him, at this psychological moment, "you can walk very well, after all. Now let us hear no more from you about being unable to walk."

If for any reason he deems the bath-tub device inadvisable, his plan is to put the child to bed, keep it entirely isolated, and deprive it of all food for a day or so. An appetising meal is then brought into the room, and left some distance from the child's bed. Frequently this is all that is needed to effect a cure. The suggestion of food overcoming the suggestion of paralysis, the child gets out of bed and starts across the room, being encountered midway by Bruns, who—of course by accident—enters the room at that precise instant, and makes use of verbal suggestion to reinforce and maintain the "miraculous" recovery.

In contrast with this method of surprise is the "method of disregard," also originated by Bruns and used by him in cases of hysteria other than those involving muscular paralysis—cases, for example, of obsessions, facial "tics," spasms, or convulsive seizures. In employing the method of disregard the little patient is carefully watched by doctor and nurses but in such a manner that he is led to believe they are paying scarcely any attention to him. As a result the idea that, despite his own conviction, his malady must be most insignificant, gradually takes increasing possession of him, and in proportion as it does so the hysterical symptoms disappear.

But, the reader may ask, does this truly mean that the hysteria itself has been cured? Do not these methods, one and all, achieve merely the removal of symptoms? Is not the child still suggestible enough to develop a new variety of hysterical disturbances should occasion arise?

Such objections are not without force, though in practice it has been observed that the cure of the symptoms by suggestion does actually seem to weaken the tendency to future hysterical outbreaks of any kind. To be on the safe side, however, it is always well to institute environmental changes of a sort that will make for a constantly closer approach by the child to a normal life.

With this, we come to the point that is of supreme interest to parents.

Almost without exception it is in the home that the seeds are sown which may afterward bear the bitter fruit of hysteria, whether bearing it in childhood or not until some critical period comes in later years. It is the child who is "spoiled," or kept by unwise parents in a state of nervous tension and excitement; the child whose sense of moral responsibility is not properly developed, and whose natural suggestibility is unduly heightened by the superstitions, fears, and eccentricities of its elders; it is such a child who, soon or late, may be counted on to manifest some hysterical taint, perhaps not of the extreme type illustrated by the cases narrated above, but nevertheless of a sort making against happiness, usefulness, and success in the world of active effort. Or, to state the situation in more detail in the words of a physician of my acquaintance:

"Hysterical children, it has been my observation, usually have neurotic parents. At first I was disposed to see in this another evidence of the dread workings of heredity. But I am now inclined to the belief that it illustrates rather the influence of environment. All children, as you know, are highly imitative. They tend to copy, with exaggerations, whatever models are placed before them, and instinctively they take their parents as their chief models. If, then, the parents are flighty, excitable, passing rapidly from extreme to extreme of mood, it is only natural that the children should be likewise. Their minds undisciplined, their will-power undeveloped, they easily fall a prey to the baneful, hysteria-producing suggestions of their unhealthy surroundings.

"To make matters worse, there is often, even among well-educated persons, an amazing disregard of the hygienic and dietetic requirements for neural stability. Children are allowed to sit up to unreasonable hours; they are permitted altogether too frequent attendance at parties, theatres, moving-picture shows, and similar places of entertainment, where they receive impressions too vivid and varied for them to absorb easily. Then, too, there is a tendency to give them at their meals an undue allowance of meat, and to permit them to drink tea, coffee, and other stimulants making for nerve disturbance.

"All the while they are living in an atmosphere of parental uneasiness and unrest. Their mothers—and perhaps their fathers also—fuss and fume over them. They delight, it may be, in 'showing them off' to admiring visitors, thus suggesting to the already over-impressionable little ones undue ideas of their own importance. Presently signs of trouble appear—restless sleep, 'night terrors,' facial 'tics,' possibly even full-blown attacks of hysterical convulsions, paralysis, deafness, or what not—and the neurologist has another patient on his hands."

Surely the duty of parents is plain. To set before their children from earliest infancy examples of placidity and strength of character, to educate their will no less than their intellect, to guard them as far as possible from all harmful suggestions, to love them without idolising them, to study carefully their physical as well as their mental and moral needs—in this way, and in this way alone, can safety be had against the dread evil of hysteria and allied nervous troubles. Especially is such a course indispensable in view of the now well-demonstrated fact that a faulty upbringing may be primarily responsible for mental and nervous maladies, not of childhood but of adult life, and of a character to challenge the utmost skill of the best trained physicians. Of this, more in our next chapter.

VIII

THE MENACE OF FEAR

I have no intention of describing the ordinary, familiar phenomena of fear. These, in both their psychological and physiological manifestations, will be found adequately treated in any good text-book on the emotions. What I wish to do, rather, is to call attention to some little-known facts which find scant mention in the text-books for the excellent reason that it is only within the past few years that they have been made part of organised knowledge. Yet they are facts of the utmost significance from both a theoretical and a practical point of view; and, indeed, an understanding of them is of no less importance to the layman than to the scientist. Their discovery has made possible for the first time what may be called an applied psychology of fear—that is to say, a statement of principles the application of which will go far toward solving the problem of how to avert the evil consequences of fear without the loss of its really beneficial qualities.

That there is a certain virtue in fear requires no scientific demonstration. Fear, as everybody ought to be aware, is intrinsically one of the most useful of emotions. It is an instinct implanted in us as a prime aid in the struggle for existence. Doubtless for this reason it is, as compared with the other emotions, the earliest to make its appearance in the newborn child. Preyer, whose book, "The Mind of the Child," is not nearly so well known in this country as it should be, puts the first manifestation of fear in an infant at the twenty-third day after birth. Other observers, including Charles Darwin, have found no indications of it until somewhat later than this. But all agree that it is the first emotion, properly so called, to show itself, and that its normal function is to instil caution and prudence in relation to objects and actions that might have destructive effects.

The trouble is that fear has a great tendency to function to excess, especially in the years of childhood, that formative period which means so much to future development. There is scarcely one of us who, looking back, cannot recall some youthful fear, abnormal in its intensity. Nor are such abnormal fears confined to the young. With many people they persist in one form or another throughout life; it may be as fear of thunder, fear of mice, fear of snakes. Moreover, they sometimes do not appear with full force until the period of youth is long past. At the age of thirty or forty—at any age—there may develop, with irresistible power, and seemingly for no reason, a paralysing, appalling fear of doing some trivial, everyday act, or of coming into contact with some familiar and entirely harmless object. When fear becomes as extreme as this it amounts to a disease, and is recognised as such by the medical profession, being technically known as a "phobia." It is through scientific study of these phobias, as recently carried out by medical specialists with a psychological training, that full realisation has been gained of the tremendous rôle played by fear in the life of man, and the need for its proper control and direction.

The two commonest phobias are direct opposites of one another—namely, fear of open places (agoraphobia) and fear of being in a closed place (claustrophobia). The victim of agoraphobia can with difficulty be persuaded to trust himself outdoors. He fears that if he goes out some catastrophe will overwhelm him. His state of mind is one of absolute panic, and when obliged to cross any open space, such as a public park, he displays all the symptoms of extreme fear. The person troubled with abnormal fear of closed places experiences no difficulty of this sort. He is, on the contrary, never so happy as when in the open. His troubles begin when he is asked to take, say, a drive in a cab or a journey in a railway car. He dare not attend the theatre, or any indoor public entertainment. Whence comes his aversion from closed places he cannot say. He only knows that the mere thought of being in any place from which he cannot escape at a moment's notice fills him with a torturing dread.

In accounting for phobias like these psychologists have, as a usual thing, fallen back on pure theory, and—especially when strongly influenced by the evolutionary doctrine—have been wont to attribute them to the emergence of ancestral traits and instincts once of real biological value. But recent investigation has made it certain that this ancestral revival theory is both superfluous and erroneous, and tends to hinder rather than help an understanding of the mechanism and consequences of fear. For one thing, there is the fact that agoraphobia and claustrophobia are not the only irrational fears. There may be a phobia for any conceivable act or object, and to explain all these in terms of the revival of ancestral instincts is surely beyond the power of the most vivid scientific imagination. Further than this, so far as abnormal fear of open or closed spaces is concerned, the researches of the medical specialists have rendered possible a satisfactory explanation—and an explanation that has much practical value—without harking back to the feelings and doings of primitive man.

It has been found in every case scientifically studied that there is indeed a memory revival of past experiences, but that it is invariably a revival of experiences in the life of the victim himself, not of his remote ancestors. This is true of every kind of phobia. The sufferer may honestly declare his inability to recall any antecedent happening of a fear-inducing character. But it is found that, subconsciously at any rate, he always carries with him a vivid memory-image of some occurrence that at the time shocked him greatly; and that his phobia is due to the ceaseless presentation in his subconsciousness of this vivid memory-image. In proof of which may be cited the experiences of any medical man accustomed, in treating patients for nervous and mental troubles, to make use of modern methods—hypnotism, hynoidisation, and so forth—for exploring the obscurer workings of the human mind.

Take, by way of illustration, a case of abnormal fear of open places successfully treated by Doctor Isador H. Coriat, a Boston neurologist of my acquaintance. The patient was a young man who for nearly two years had been tormented by an irrational fear of fields, parks, and public squares. His relatives and friends had argued with him, he had tried to conquer the phobia by force of will, but all to no purpose. Nor could he give any reason for his abnormal dread.

Put into the hypnotic state, however, and questioned again, he recalled an incident that at once revealed its source. Two years previously, it appeared, he had been taking a horseback ride, when he unexpectedly galloped into an open field.

"I became terribly frightened," said he, "as the ground was rough, and I thought I should certainly fall off the horse. I felt faint, my heart beat rapidly, I broke into a cold perspiration and trembled all over. It seemed as if the end of the world was coming. Since then, whenever I see a field or a park I am reminded of this, and feel the same agonising fear."

In the case of another patient suffering from fear of closed spaces the abnormal fear was traced to an occasion when, visiting a friend in a small, close room, the patient had a fainting attack. In a third patient, a young woman, there developed a fear of crowds because, some time previously, at a crowded school celebration, she had been slightly overcome by heat, and had "felt like screaming." Another young woman was afflicted with pyrophobia, or fear of fire, in such an extreme form that she could not remain in a room where an open fire was burning, and every night made the rounds of her house to satisfy herself there was nothing that could start a conflagration. Inquiry showed that all this morbid anxiety was an outgrowth of a previous experience with fire.

Sometimes memory of the antecedent causal experience is not entirely blotted out of the upper consciousness. The sufferer may even entertain a clear recollection of it and still be unable to conquer his phobia; which, however, under these circumstances is not nearly so severe as when the process is entirely one of subconscious mentation. In either case, of course, the problem of the development of the phobia still requires explanation. Only partial enlightenment is gained, after all, when we recognise the causal action of some specific occurrence, such as a fall, a fainting-fit, or the sight of a fire. Thousands of persons experience these things without thereby becoming victims of a phobia. When a phobia does result, some exceptional circumstances must be operative, and it is manifestly desirable to learn, if possible, what these are.

It is the more desirable since, as investigation is daily revealing more and more clearly, abnormal dread is not the only malady resulting from a fear-occasioning event. Where one man, as the result of a sudden fright, may in course of time become a phobiac, another may develop symptoms, not of mental trouble, but of bodily disease. A most instructive instance is afforded by the experiences of a young Russian immigrant in this country who had the good fortune to come under the observation of those two eminent specialists in the treatment of mentally-caused disorders, Doctors Morton Prince and Boris Sidis.

The trouble for which this young man sought relief was, to all appearance, purely physical. It consisted of periodic convulsive attacks that racked the right half of his body, and had led to a diagnosis of epilepsy. Since sundry delicate symptoms characteristic of epilepsy were absent, however, the specialists, after a careful study of the case, came to the conclusion that the spasms from which their patient suffered might involve no true organic disease, and might be nothing more than the outward manifestation of some deep-seated psychical disturbance. With this possibility in mind they questioned him both in the normal waking state and in hypnosis, and brought to light some interesting facts.

The first attack, he told them, had set in five years before, when he was sixteen years old and living in Russia. After returning from a dance one evening, he went back to look for a ring lost by the young lady whom he had escorted home. It was past midnight, and his way lay over a country road by a cemetery. Nearing the cemetery, he thought he heard somebody or something running after him. He turned to flee, fell, and lost consciousness. He still was unconscious when found on the road. After he had been brought to, it was seen that he was afflicted with a spasmodic, uncontrollable shaking of the right side, involving his head, arm, and leg. This lasted almost a week, when he seemed as well as ever. But every year thereafter, at about the same time, he had had an attack similar in all respects to the first one, excepting only that he did not become unconscious.

He further declared, while in the hypnotic state, that throughout the period of the attacks he had unpleasant dreams, all relating to the fright and fall of five years before. In these dreams he lived over and over again the experience from which his trouble dated.

"I find myself," said he, "on the lonely road in my little native town. I am hurrying along the road near the cemetery. It is very dark. I imagine somebody—a robber, or a ghost—is running after me. I become frightened, call for help, and fall. Then I wake up with a start, and remember nothing about the dream. I no longer am afraid, but I have these terrible spasms."

It was even found possible to produce the convulsive attacks experimentally by simply reminding him, while hypnotised, of the incident on the road. To Doctors Prince and Sidis it now seemed certain that his malady was due to nothing else than the persistence of an intensely vivid subconscious memory-image of the fright he had experienced; and that he would no longer be troubled by it if the memory-image were destroyed by psychotherapeutic treatment. Suggestions to this effect were accordingly given him, when awake as well as when hypnotised. The outcome was all that could be desired, for a speedy and permanent cure was brought about.

Paralysis, muscular contractures, symptoms mimicking tuberculosis, kidney disease, and other dread organic maladies, are also recognised to-day as possible after-effects, through the power of subconscious mental action, of happenings that give rise to a profound feeling of fear. Sometimes more than one symptom is thus occasioned in the same patient. Again, for the purpose of concrete illustration, I cite a typical case from real life—the case of a Pole, a man of twenty-five, treated for a weird combination of mental and physical disturbances.

Physically, he suffered from severe and frequent attacks of headache, setting in gradually, and preceded by a feeling of depression and dizziness. During the attacks his body became cold, his head throbbed violently, he shivered incessantly. To keep warm, he was obliged to wrap himself in many blankets. Mentally, he was tormented by many phobias. He was afraid of closed places, and still more afraid of being obliged to remain alone, especially at night. He had a morbid fear of the dead, and would on no account enter a room with a corpse in it or attend a funeral. Nothing could induce him to visit a cemetery, even in company with other people. Fear of dogs was also a conspicuous feature of his case, as was fear of fire.

Through psychological exploration of his subconsciousness, every one of these symptoms was traced to actual experiences that had given him great emotional shocks, and in almost every instance to experiences that had occurred in his childhood. The fear of dogs had its origin in an exciting episode he had had with some dogs when he was only three. The pyrophobia was connected with the fact that at four years of age he had been hastily carried from a burning building, shivering with fright and cold, into the open air of a frosty night. His dread of cemeteries and of the dead was rooted in a subconscious recollection of terrors inspired in him, while a child, by hearing "all kinds of ghost stories and tales of wandering lost souls, and of spirits of dead people hovering about churchyards."

In addition to this, his mother, a very superstitious woman, when he was nine, placed the cold hand of a corpse on his naked chest as a "cure" for some trifling ailment. Hence his special fear of corpses. As to the headaches and the sensations of cold, they were the result partly of this "dead hand" memory, and partly of the memory of a still more severe experience, occurring at about the same time, when he was forced to spend an entire night in a barn in mid-winter, to escape a party of drunken soldiers who had beaten his father unmercifully and had killed one of his little brothers. His fear of closed spaces and his fear of being alone were associated with the same experience.

As he grew older much of all this faded from his conscious recollection. But, by analysing his dreams and questioning him in hypnosis, it was found that subconsciously he had forgotten none of it. Evidence also was forthcoming indicating that from time to time, owing to the occurrence of later experiences of a less sinister nature but disquieting enough, there had been exceptionally vivid revivals of the earlier memories; and that it was in this way that they had been able to acquire such tremendous disease-producing power.

Here, I am confident, we have the answer to the question raised in connection with the development of phobias in adult life from seemingly trivial occurrences. Heredity, no doubt, plays some part. But assuredly a far greater influence is exercised by the presence of baneful memory-images that need only an appropriate stimulus to excite them into pernicious activity. The mechanism of fear-caused diseases, to put it briefly, is probably much the same as that operating in the production of the familiar phenomenon of dreaming.

When we dream of anything, we do so because an incident of the waking life has, through association of ideas, roused some dormant emotional "complex," some group of subconscious ideas relating to matters which are, or once were, of great significance to us, and our dream is a symbolic expression of this dormant complex.[4] So is it with the man who suffers from a fear-induced malady, whether it take the form of a mental or of a physical disorder.

Perhaps of a neurotic tendency by inheritance, perhaps of a good heredity, but temporarily weakened by grief, worry, etc., something occurs that gives this person a sudden fright, and, by association of ideas, reminds him, if only subconsciously, of earlier fear-inspiring episodes in his life. Ordinarily there would be no unpleasant after-effect, except possibly a few nights of bad dreams. But in his condition dreaming is not sufficient to give vent to the subconscious emotions. Some other channel of discharge must be found, and it is found in the production of disease-symptoms—whether mental or physical, or both mental and physical—symbolising the emotional complex or complexes stimulated by the happening that frightened him.

Indeed, there is reason for suspecting that all functional nervous and mental troubles, no matter what their immediate cause, are traceable to fear-memories of remote occurrence, dating usually from the days of childhood. Certainly it is possible to detail from recent medical practice innumerable cases in support of this view. Not to be tedious, I will give only one or two, selecting first a case of Doctor Coriat's, in which the patient, a middle-aged woman, had for years been tormented by an increasing fear that she would go insane, and that, if insane, she would inevitably injure some member of her family. The poor woman had worn herself out brooding over this, and was gradually qualifying for commitment to some institution. But Doctor Coriat could not find, either in her physical condition or in the facts of her family history, anything to warrant her belief that she was doomed to become insane.

Suspecting, therefore, that this belief was merely a hysterical outgrowth of some forgotten shock in her previous life, and knowing that in sleep such latent memories have a tendency to emerge momentarily into the field of consciousness, he questioned her regarding the frequency and content of her dreams.

"I dream a great deal," she told him, "but I never have a clear remembrance of what I have dreamed about."

Yet, when hypnotised and again questioned regarding the dreams, she was able to detail many of them. One in particular interested Doctor Coriat. It was of a recurrent character, and was identified by the patient as having first been dreamed at the time she began to worry over her condition. It was, in fact, a dream in which she saw herself insane.

"Had anything unpleasant happened to you the day before you first had that dream?" Doctor Coriat now inquired of his hypnotised patient.

"Nothing that I can remember, except that I went to a friend's funeral."

"The funeral of a very dear friend?"

"Not exactly—just a friend."

"But that should not have had such a disturbing effect on your mind. Did anything happen at the funeral?"

"I saw a woman there whose eyes frightened me."

"And why did they frighten you?"

"Because they reminded me of a preacher I used to know when I was a little girl. He was a revivalist, and I always thought he was crazy. I went to his meetings, and got terribly worked up, and it frightened me very much. I thought I would go crazy too, just like the preacher."

To Doctor Coriat it seemed unnecessary to ask any more questions. As he saw it, the haunting dread of insanity was nothing but the continuation in consciousness of the forgotten memory of the childhood fright, revived by subconscious association of the woman at the funeral with the preacher whose rabid exhortations had inspired the patient with such terror. On this theory he utilised the resources of medical psychology to deprive the baneful memory-image of its power to harm, and soon had the satisfaction of being able to record a perfect cure.

In another case, successfully treated by Doctor Sidis, the subconscious persistence of childhood fears actually threatened a young woman with perhaps lifelong confinement in an asylum for the insane. She had, in fact, been placed in a New York hospital for observation, and it was there that Doctor Sidis treated her. According to her relatives, who did not doubt that she had lost her reason, she suffered from strange hallucinations, particularly of constantly hearing voices call to her, and of being killed. She even imagined at times that she was dead, and would lie in a cataleptic condition, rigidly motionless. At other times she complained of a painful stiffness in her arms, and of difficulty in walking.

Testing her psychologically, Doctor Sidis found cause for thinking that her trouble was hysterical rather than a true insanity involving brain lesions, and he promptly questioned her relatives regarding her previous history. She had had, he learned, some exceedingly unpleasant experiences with a brother-in-law, a rough, brutal fellow, but they did not seem adequate to account for her various symptoms. These, he suspected, had their roots farther back in her life, and, although she professed a total inability to recall any severe fright or worry other than those associated with her brother-in-law, he remained unshaken in his suspicion.

"What do you dream about?" he asked her.

"I don't exactly know," she replied. "I am sure I dream a good deal, though, for when I wake I always seem to have been dreaming, and to have had horrid dreams. All I can say is that I dimly remember seeing in them many ugly faces."

"Is your brother-in-law's face among them?"

"Yes, and other people's faces. But I'm sure I don't know who they are."

Subjected to a special process of "mind tunneling" of Doctor Sidis's own invention, the patient recalled a number of dreams in vivid detail. Most of them showed a strong resemblance to one another, in that they had as their setting a forest, and as their chief actors men of repulsive aspect, usually dressed in the roughest of clothing, and usually intent on capturing the dreamer. Only the night before, she declared, she had dreamed that a man was trying to choke her, and she had awakened panic-stricken, and so drenched with perspiration that her nurse—who corroborated her statement—had had to change her night-gown.

"Can you identify the men of your dreams—the men dressed in rough clothing who pursue you so fiercely?" Doctor Sidis asked, while she still was in the artificial state into which he had put her.

"Yes, yes," she answered, much agitated. "I know them only too well."

Now, for the first time, she related to him two most significant episodes of her girlhood. Once, it appeared, when she was hardly nine years old, she was walking along a country road, past a forest, when a wood-cutter—"a big man, with big arms and hands projecting from short sleeves"—tried to catch her and carry her into the forest. "He ran after me with outstretched arms. I screamed, and ran from him as fast as I could, calling for help all the time." And, on another occasion, when she was even younger—only six—on her way to school through the woods, a man met her, gave her candy, talked to her nicely, and all at once seized her so roughly that she began to scream with fright and pain. At that moment somebody came along, and the man released her and fled.

These were the men whom she chiefly saw in her dreams; these were the shocks which, aggravated by the more recent experiences of a not dissimilar sort with her brother-in-law, were the true determinants of her hysteria—as was proved by the fact that upon psychological disintegration of her subconscious memories of them, a speedy and lasting return to health resulted.

In like manner the seemingly epileptic attacks of a nineteen-year-old New York "street arab" were found to be nothing more than the external manifestation of subconscious memory-images, dating back to early childhood, of nights passed in a dark, damp, terror-inspiring cellar. The sight of the discoloured corpse of a man who had died from cholera left in the mind of a sensitive girl of ten such a painful impression that years afterward, quite unaccountably as it seemed, she developed an abnormal fear of contracting some deadly disease; and had she not fortunately been taken to a skilled medical psychologist (Doctor Pierre Janet) she would almost certainly have ended her days in an asylum. In the case of an overworked Boston young man, thought to be suffering from "dementia praecox," it was found that his morbid notion that he had committed an "unpardonable sin" was only a hysterical product of subconsciously remembered fears of childhood. The victim himself eventually recognised this, declaring, in an autobiographical statement made at his physician's request:

"My abnormal fear certainly originated from doctrines of hell which I heard in early childhood, particularly from a rather ignorant elderly woman who taught Sunday-school. My early religious thought was chiefly concerned with the direful eternity of torture that might be awaiting me if I was not good enough to be saved."

Whether or no all cases of functional nervous and mental disease are thus rooted in emotional stresses of youth, certainly this is often enough the fact to constitute a serious warning to all who have anything to do with the upbringing of the young. If fears of childhood can persist throughout life and can affect adult development so profoundly as to be causal agents in the production of disease, it is obvious that parents and educators should adopt every means in their power to prevent the growth of unreasonable fears in the little ones in their care. Yet, as matters are to-day, and not least in the home, most children are subject to influences that tend to foster, not inhibit, such fears.

In their presence, as was noted on a previous page, parents often discuss accidents, crimes, sensational doings of all sorts; they betray a fretfulness, an anxiety, an unrest, that cannot but react on the sensitive mind of the child, filling it with fears of it knows not what; they even utilise the fear impulse as a means of coercing the child into good behaviour; and, what is perhaps worst of all, many parents intrust their children to ignorant and superstitious nurses, who take a strange pleasure in "scaring them half to death" with tales of demons, ghosts and goblins.

Fortunately the majority of people, as a result of later training and experience, or by the exercise of will-power, are able to suppress the fears of childhood; but often only at the cost of great mental torture. Not so long ago I received a letter from a Detroit business man, Mr. John J. Mitchell, that may well be quoted in this connection. He wrote:

"As a child, as far back as memory goes, I was 'afraid of the dark,' intensely afraid.... At about eleven years of age I got a place in a country store, and perhaps two years later changed to the largest store in town. This concern did a large, old-fashioned country business, buying produce and selling all manner of merchandise in exchange or on credit. This involved the use of two old-time buildings (frame) with three stories each and a cellar under all. Owing to the character of the business and location, there were doors opening to the street and area on each side and rear from every floor, including the cellar, seven or eight in all, and widely apart, besides windows. It was my duty at dusk to see that all these doors were properly closed and barred for the night.... With my childish fear of the dark this daily task was an ordeal—at times a terrible ordeal.

"I never made complaint or confided my fears to a soul. But for some reason, the source of which was, and is, as obscure as my intangible fears, I resolved to cure myself of this terror.... My plan, adopted and unflinchingly carried out, was to compel myself—a slender, timid little kid—to go that round daily, in the shadowy dusk, without a light (which I was privileged to have, a lantern). I can only remember now the *pain* of dread and unreasoning apprehension, and the resolution to 'have it over and done with.'

"I cannot now fix the time when it was accomplished, but in the end I was completely cured, so that, at least since my majority, I have not only been relieved of this dread, but I often welcome the folds of darkness (of night), as if wrapped about with a comforting garment. It will be a certain qualification to state that, at very long intervals, and always after some physical or mental strain, I feel momentarily a fear of return of old impressions in 'uncanny' surroundings."

And, beyond any question, no matter how effectually one may suppress such youthful fears, so far as relates to their survival in the upper consciousness, there will always be a subconscious remnant, a buried complex, ready to emerge and work mischief in one way or another. There is a world of truth in Professor Angelo Mosso's emphatic declaration:

"Every ugly thing told to the child, every shock, every fright given him, will remain like minute splinters in the flesh, to torture him all his life long."

If not in such an extreme form as a phobia, or other functional disease, the early fears will nevertheless make their presence felt in later life. In some men they may engender lack of self-confidence, and even a despicable cowardice; in others they may breed superstitious terrors and usages. Always, in some way, one may depend on it, they will affect the character, the intellect, the whole moral and mental make-up.

Nor will their influence be confined to the individual. Fear, as every psychologist knows, is one of the most contagious of the emotions. Socially, as well as individually, it has a useful function to perform. The presence in all civilised communities of police and fire departments, boards of health, and the like, testifies impressively to the influence of social fear working normally as a conserving agent. But there may be, and frequently is, social as well as individual abnormality of fear; as in panics, massacres, lynchings. In order to deal with this effectually, in order to keep social fear within the bounds of reason, it will always be necessary to recognise that, after all, society is made up of a mass of individuals, and can only think and feel and act as individuals think and feel and act. Train the individual properly, and society will be sane and healthy and efficient enough.

IX

A FEW CLOSING WORDS

We have now reviewed in some detail the principal results of recent psychological research and observation, so far as these bear directly on man's mental and moral growth. Varied as is the mass of information thus brought together, we have found it pointing uniformly to one conclusion—the transcendent significance of the environmental influences of early life.

Again and again we have found confirmation of the view that what a man is and does depends, as a rule, not so much on the gifts or defects of his heredity as on the excellences or shortcomings of his childhood's training and surroundings. If these are favourable, even the dead hand of a bad inheritance may be arrested, and he may develop surprising strength of intellect and character; if unfavourable, mental and moral inferiority may be looked for, no matter how good the heredity.

This, of course, emphasises the responsibilities of parenthood, chief among which, as would appear from the facts surveyed, are the beginning of formal education in the home, the providing of a carefully planned material environment, and the setting of a really good example. There can be no doubt, to return for a moment to the superlatively instructive case of Karl Witte, that by all odds the greatest force in the moral development of that splendid scholar and gentleman, was the unceasing inspiration he unconsciously drew from the lives of his father and mother—from their integrity, unselfishness, patience, sincerity, and courage. Parents cannot too soon learn that, to quote a cardinal clause in the elder Witte's educational creed:

"Our children are what we are. They are good when we are good, and bad when we are bad. I would extend this assertion. With full conviction I would say, they become clever, magnanimous, modest, witty, agreeable, amiable, if these are our qualities. They become the opposite if we precede them with the opposite."

Or, as Doctor Dubois has so admirably put it in one of his University of Berne addresses on moral education:

"You, madam, who complain of the irritability of your little girl, could you not suppress your own, which I have seen break out, in a few words exchanged with your dear husband, immediately afterward? You, sir, who bitterly reproach your son for his impulsiveness and instability of temper, have you not these faults yourself?... Remember the proverb, 'The fruit does not fall far from the tree.'" ("Reason and Sentiment," pp. 53–54.)

Personally, also, I am of Witte's belief that intellectual training along the lines followed by him in his son's upbringing is of itself an important adjunct to moral growth. Certainly, by developing the powers of observation, analysis, and inference, it makes it easier for the child to appreciate the force of any arguments advanced by the parent in the way of direct moral instruction. Besides this, by keeping the child's mind occupied with wholesome and profitable matters, it saves him from the idleness and waste of energy which, in childhood as much as in adult life, favour the formation of bad habits. And assuredly the methods by which his mental education may best be carried on in the first years of existence are such that they may be readily applied by all parents.

It is by no means a difficult thing to begin, as Witte did, by naming to the little one various small objects in and about the home. These should be named over and over to him, slowly, clearly, impressively; and the attempt should next be made to convey to him a notion of their properties, by teaching him, for example, to detect differences in colour and in such qualities as hot and cold, round and square, hard and soft, rough and smooth. This can be done in any one of several ways, but the best method, it seems to me, is that developed within recent years by the noted Italian educator of little children, Maria Montessori.

Her plan with every child whose education is intrusted to her is to start by teaching it to distinguish between various touch sensations; and she does this so successfully that her pupils, aged from three to seven, are able, blindfolded, to state the differences in extremely fine gradations of cloths, papers, coins, and seeds. Any parent can do the same thing, beginning by drilling the child in distinguishing between massive sensations, and gradually developing delicacy of touch.

Two cards, one rough, one smooth, afford an excellent starting-point. The child touches the smooth card. "Smooth," says the parent, and "Smooth" responds the child. The little fingers are then placed on the card with the rough surface. "Rough," the child is told, and "Rough" he repeats. Only a few lessons of this sort will be found necessary to enable him to select at request the smooth or the rough card and hand it to the parent. Ideas of shape, size, etc., may be similarly imparted, with the triple advantage that the child will daily, and without mental stress, acquire a more and more retentive muscular memory, a more intimate acquaintance with the facts of the world in which he lives, and greater observational and reasoning ability.

Meanwhile, of course, the fertilisation of the child's mind should also be continued by other educative measures—as the maintenance of an inspiring environment, ready and intelligent response to the child's innumerable questions, and skilful guidance of his thoughts to subjects which it is especially desirable for him to study. The system of walks and talks, utilised alike by James Thomson, James Mill, and Pastor Witte, is particularly to be recommended in this connection, as also Witte's practice of propounding to his son interesting problems, and then taking him to places—factories, mills, etc.—where he could observe for himself different stages in their solution.

Something of the same sort is possible to every parent, who can include in such voyages of discovery, if he be a city dweller, visits to botanical and zoölogical gardens, art and industrial museums, and similar institutions where his child can obtain entertainment, some insight into the workings of natural laws, and elementary instruction in subjects which will inevitably form part of his school curriculum at a later day.

But, it may be objected, does not all this mean that in order to make sure of results the father and mother will have to give the greater part of their time to the child's education? Not at all. One hour or so a day will be quite enough in the way of direct, personal tuition. And even if the task of instruction were really burdensome, surely, in view of the findings of modern science, parents will do well to keep in mind, and recognize the profound truth of, Rousseau's stern pronouncement:

"He who cannot fulfil the duties of a father has no right to be a father. Not poverty, nor severe labour, nor human respect can release him from the duty of supporting his children and of educating them himself. Readers, you may believe my words. I prophesy to any one who has natural feeling and neglects these sacred duties—that he will long shed bitter tears over this fault, and that for these tears he will find no consolation."